T0164654

# In Shakespeare's, In Shakespeare's Shadow Shadow

A Collection of *Sonnets*

Maria Tucciarone

Order this book online at www.trafford.com
or email orders@trafford.com

Most Trafford titles are also available at major online book retailers.

Printed in the United States of America.

ISBN: 978-1-4269-8747-2 (sc)
ISBN: 978-1-4269-8256-9 (hc)
ISBN: 978-1-4269-8748-9 (e)

Library of Congress Control Number: 2011915655

*Trafford rev. 09/23/2011*

 www.trafford.com

North America & international
toll-free: 1 888 232 4444 (USA & Canada)
phone: 250 383 6864 ♦ fax: 812 355 4082

To Betty Jaffee, my high school English teacher, who taught me the love of language, the power of poetry, and the immortality and soulfulness of the sonnet.

"And as imagination bodies forth
The form of things unknown, the poet's pen
Turns them to shapes, and gives to airy nothing
A local habitation and a name."

A Midsummer Night's Dream, V,i,4.

~ William Shakespeare

# Table of Contents

# SONNETS

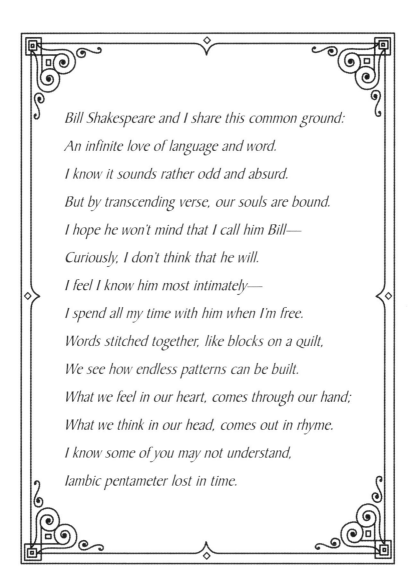

*Bill Shakespeare and I share this common ground:*

*An infinite love of language and word.*

*I know it sounds rather odd and absurd.*

*But by transcending verse, our souls are bound.*

*I hope he won't mind that I call him Bill—*

*Curiously, I don't think that he will.*

*I feel I know him most intimately—*

*I spend all my time with him when I'm free.*

*Words stitched together, like blocks on a quilt,*

*We see how endless patterns can be built.*

*What we feel in our heart, comes through our hand;*

*What we think in our head, comes out in rhyme.*

*I know some of you may not understand,*

*Iambic pentameter lost in time.*

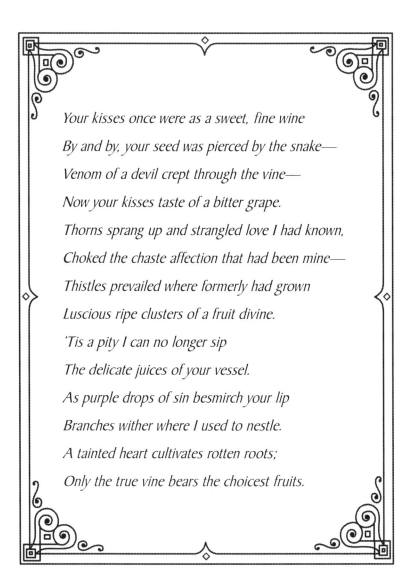

Your kisses once were as a sweet, fine wine
By and by, your seed was pierced by the snake—
Venom of a devil crept through the vine—
Now your kisses taste of a bitter grape.
Thorns sprang up and strangled love I had known,
Choked the chaste affection that had been mine—
Thistles prevailed where formerly had grown
Luscious ripe clusters of a fruit divine.
'Tis a pity I can no longer sip
The delicate juices of your vessel.
As purple drops of sin besmirch your lip
Branches wither where I used to nestle.
A tainted heart cultivates rotten roots;
Only the true vine bears the choicest fruits.

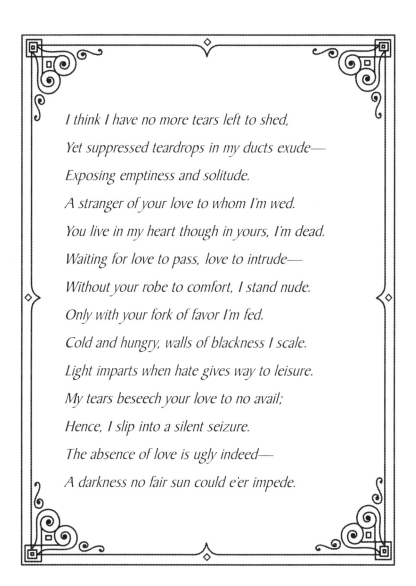

*I think I have no more tears left to shed,*

*Yet suppressed teardrops in my ducts exude—*

*Exposing emptiness and solitude.*

*A stranger of your love to whom I'm wed.*

*You live in my heart though in yours, I'm dead.*

*Waiting for love to pass, love to intrude—*

*Without your robe to comfort, I stand nude.*

*Only with your fork of favor I'm fed.*

*Cold and hungry, walls of blackness I scale.*

*Light imparts when hate gives way to leisure.*

*My tears beseech your love to no avail;*

*Hence, I slip into a silent seizure.*

*The absence of love is ugly indeed—*

*A darkness no fair sun could e'er impede.*

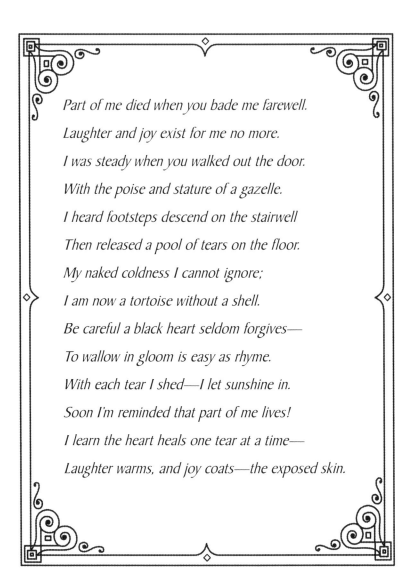

*Part of me died when you bade me farewell.*

*Laughter and joy exist for me no more.*

*I was steady when you walked out the door.*

*With the poise and stature of a gazelle.*

*I heard footsteps descend on the stairwell*

*Then released a pool of tears on the floor.*

*My naked coldness I cannot ignore;*

*I am now a tortoise without a shell.*

*Be careful a black heart seldom forgives—*

*To wallow in gloom is easy as rhyme.*

*With each tear I shed—I let sunshine in.*

*Soon I'm reminded that part of me lives!*

*I learn the heart heals one tear at a time—*

*Laughter warms, and joy coats—the exposed skin.*

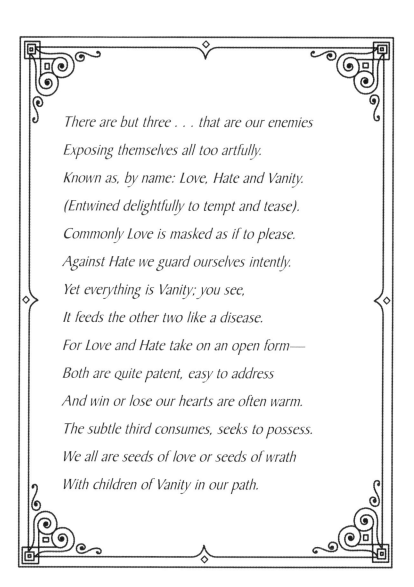

*There are but three . . . that are our enemies*

*Exposing themselves all too artfully.*

*Known as, by name: Love, Hate and Vanity.*

*(Entwined delightfully to tempt and tease).*

*Commonly Love is masked as if to please.*

*Against Hate we guard ourselves intently.*

*Yet everything is Vanity; you see,*

*It feeds the other two like a disease.*

*For Love and Hate take on an open form—*

*Both are quite patent, easy to address*

*And win or lose our hearts are often warm.*

*The subtle third consumes, seeks to possess.*

*We all are seeds of love or seeds of wrath*

*With children of Vanity in our path.*

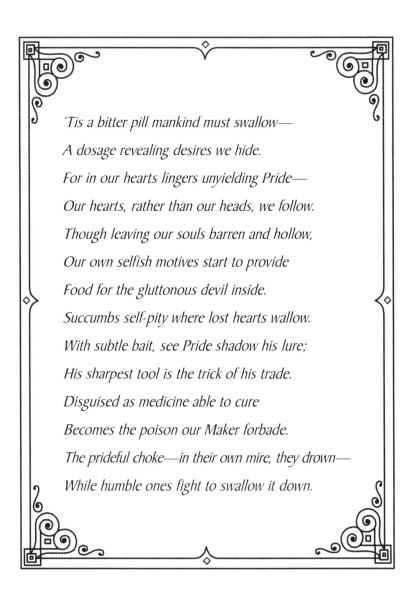

*'Tis a bitter pill mankind must swallow—*
*A dosage revealing desires we hide.*
*For in our hearts lingers unyielding Pride—*
*Our hearts, rather than our heads, we follow.*
*Though leaving our souls barren and hollow,*
*Our own selfish motives start to provide*
*Food for the gluttonous devil inside.*
*Succumbs self-pity where lost hearts wallow.*
*With subtle bait, see Pride shadow his lure;*
*His sharpest tool is the trick of his trade.*
*Disguised as medicine able to cure*
*Becomes the poison our Maker forbade.*
*The prideful choke—in their own mire, they drown—*
*While humble ones fight to swallow it down.*

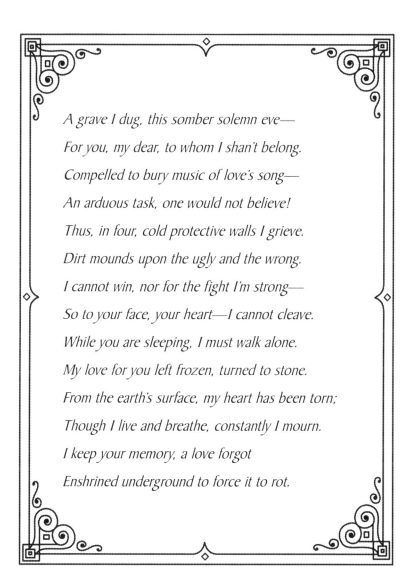

*A grave I dug, this somber solemn eve—*

*For you, my dear, to whom I shan't belong.*

*Compelled to bury music of love's song—*

*An arduous task, one would not believe!*

*Thus, in four, cold protective walls I grieve.*

*Dirt mounds upon the ugly and the wrong.*

*I cannot win, nor for the fight I'm strong—*

*So to your face, your heart—I cannot cleave.*

*While you are sleeping, I must walk alone.*

*My love for you left frozen, turned to stone.*

*From the earth's surface, my heart has been torn;*

*Though I live and breathe, constantly I mourn.*

*I keep your memory, a love forgot*

*Enshrined underground to force it to rot.*

Come winter, you are freshly fallen flakes

Of snow, dancing upon my face like dew.

Though green is gone you waken death anew.

As spring enters and with her life awakes

Every garden and flower she may meet.

With each bud bloom—so does my love for you.

In summer's sky ablaze with shades of blue—

Her sultry air reeks your aroma sweet.

The fields, the sun's heart, randomly does blanch

Whilst your colors kaleidoscope my mind.

The autumn leaves cling firmly to the branch

And I to your love of the harvest kind.

As thunder to storm—as thoughts to reason:

So you are ripe love, always in season.

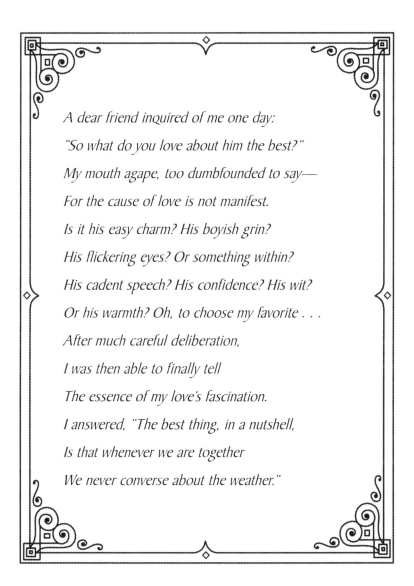

A dear friend inquired of me one day:

"So what do you love about him the best?"

My mouth agape, too dumbfounded to say—

For the cause of love is not manifest.

Is it his easy charm? His boyish grin?

His flickering eyes? Or something within?

His cadent speech? His confidence? His wit?

Or his warmth? Oh, to choose my favorite . . .

After much careful deliberation,

I was then able to finally tell

The essence of my love's fascination.

I answered, "The best thing, in a nutshell,

Is that whenever we are together

We never converse about the weather."

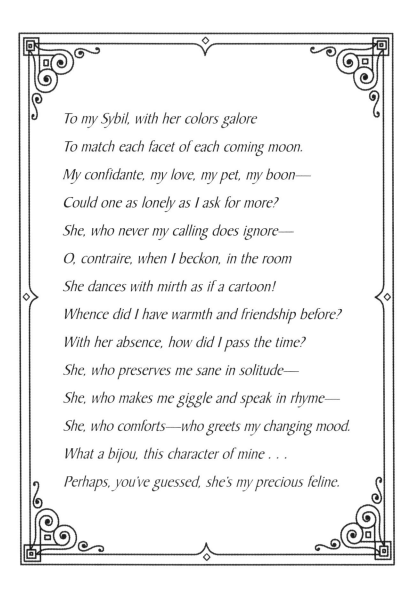

To my Sybil, with her colors galore

To match each facet of each coming moon.

My confidante, my love, my pet, my boon—

Could one as lonely as I ask for more?

She, who never my calling does ignore—

O, contraire, when I beckon, in the room

She dances with mirth as if a cartoon!

Whence did I have warmth and friendship before?

With her absence, how did I pass the time?

She, who preserves me sane in solitude—

She, who makes me giggle and speak in rhyme—

She, who comforts—who greets my changing mood.

What a bijou, this character of mine . . .

Perhaps, you've guessed, she's my precious feline.

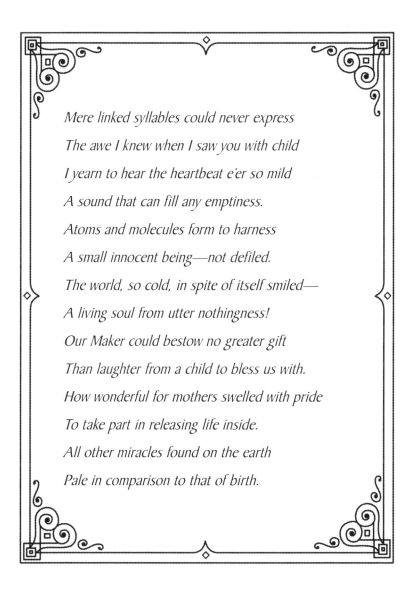

*Mere linked syllables could never express*

*The awe I knew when I saw you with child*

*I yearn to hear the heartbeat e'er so mild*

*A sound that can fill any emptiness.*

*Atoms and molecules form to harness*

*A small innocent being—not defiled.*

*The world, so cold, in spite of itself smiled—*

*A living soul from utter nothingness!*

*Our Maker could bestow no greater gift*

*Than laughter from a child to bless us with.*

*How wonderful for mothers swelled with pride*

*To take part in releasing life inside.*

*All other miracles found on the earth*

*Pale in comparison to that of birth.*

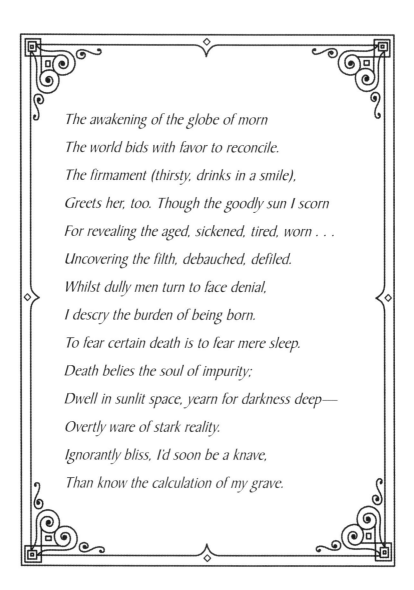

The awakening of the globe of morn
The world bids with favor to reconcile.
The firmament (thirsty, drinks in a smile),
Greets her, too. Though the goodly sun I scorn
For revealing the aged, sickened, tired, worn . . .
Uncovering the filth, debauched, defiled.
Whilst dully men turn to face denial,
I descry the burden of being born.
To fear certain death is to fear mere sleep.
Death belies the soul of impurity;
Dwell in sunlit space, yearn for darkness deep—
Overtly ware of stark reality.
Ignorantly bliss, I'd soon be a knave,
Than know the calculation of my grave.

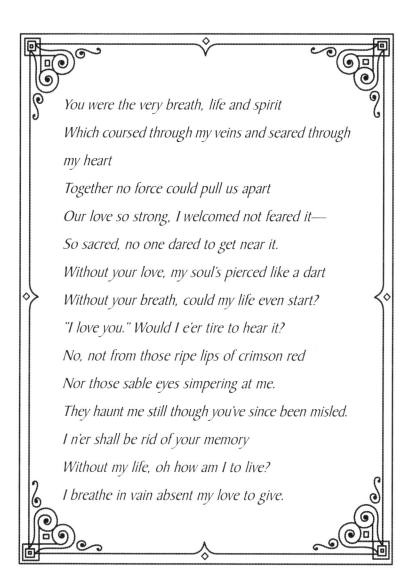

You were the very breath, life and spirit

Which coursed through my veins and seared through

my heart

Together no force could pull us apart

Our love so strong, I welcomed not feared it—

So sacred, no one dared to get near it.

Without your love, my soul's pierced like a dart

Without your breath, could my life even start?

"I love you." Would I e'er tire to hear it?

No, not from those ripe lips of crimson red

Nor those sable eyes simpering at me.

They haunt me still though you've since been misled.

I n'er shall be rid of your memory

Without my life, oh how am I to live?

I breathe in vain absent my love to give.

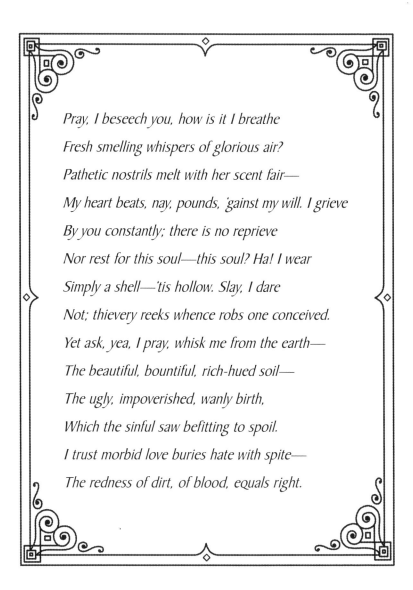

*Pray, I beseech you, how is it I breathe*

*Fresh smelling whispers of glorious air?*

*Pathetic nostrils melt with her scent fair—*

*My heart beats, nay, pounds, 'gainst my will. I grieve*

*By you constantly; there is no reprieve*

*Nor rest for this soul—this soul? Ha! I wear*

*Simply a shell—'tis hollow. Slay, I dare*

*Not; thievery reeks whence robs one conceived.*

*Yet ask, yea, I pray, whisk me from the earth—*

*The beautiful, bountiful, rich-hued soil—*

*The ugly, impoverished, wanly birth,*

*Which the sinful saw befitting to spoil.*

*I trust morbid love buries hate with spite—*

*The redness of dirt, of blood, equals right.*

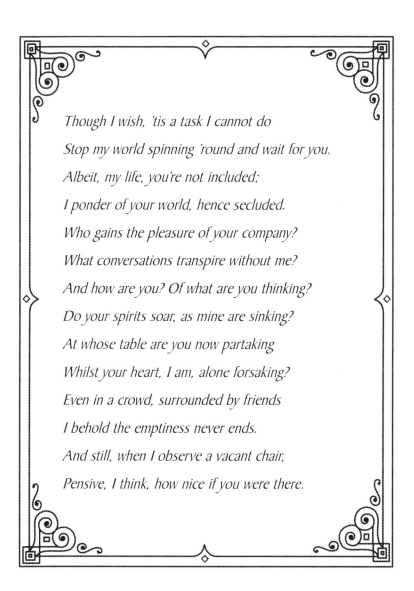

*Though I wish, 'tis a task I cannot do*

*Stop my world spinning 'round and wait for you.*

*Albeit, my life, you're not included;*

*I ponder of your world, hence secluded.*

*Who gains the pleasure of your company?*

*What conversations transpire without me?*

*And how are you? Of what are you thinking?*

*Do your spirits soar, as mine are sinking?*

*At whose table are you now partaking*

*Whilst your heart, I am, alone forsaking?*

*Even in a crowd, surrounded by friends*

*I behold the emptiness never ends.*

*And still, when I observe a vacant chair,*

*Pensive, I think, how nice if you were there.*

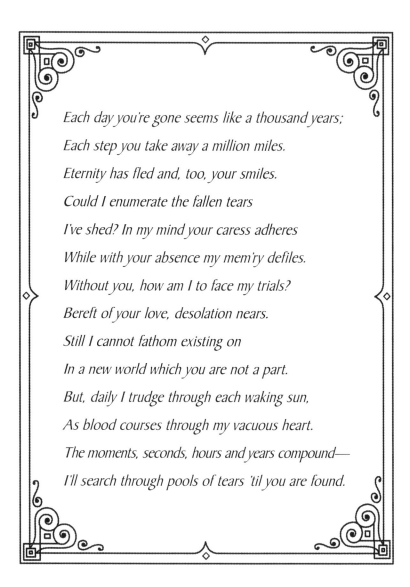

Each day you're gone seems like a thousand years;

Each step you take away a million miles.

Eternity has fled and, too, your smiles.

Could I enumerate the fallen tears

I've shed? In my mind your caress adheres

While with your absence my mem'ry defiles.

Without you, how am I to face my trials?

Bereft of your love, desolation nears.

Still I cannot fathom existing on

In a new world which you are not a part.

But, daily I trudge through each waking sun,

As blood courses through my vacuous heart.

The moments, seconds, hours and years compound—

I'll search through pools of tears 'til you are found.

*It is odd . . . your very soul consumes mine.*

*I marvel in my mind the reason why.*

*I cannot dismiss you, although I try.*

*How I am smitten, I cannot define—*

*Yet your face is before me all the time.*

*I see your image, even when I lie*

*Asleep at night as the stars saunter by.*

*While awake it is for your heart I pine.*

*Like a phantom, you haunt even my step.*

*I rationally attempt to discern*

*Whence you possessed the deep secret I kept?*

*In vain, I hanker for the day I learn*

*The maddening mystery, so I wait*

*And pray the answer does not come too late.*

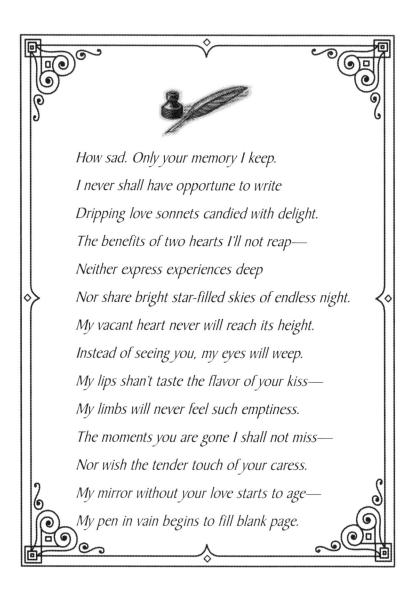

How sad. Only your memory I keep.

I never shall have opportune to write

Dripping love sonnets candied with delight.

The benefits of two hearts I'll not reap—

Neither express experiences deep

Nor share bright star-filled skies of endless night.

My vacant heart never will reach its height.

Instead of seeing you, my eyes will weep.

My lips shan't taste the flavor of your kiss—

My limbs will never feel such emptiness.

The moments you are gone I shall not miss—

Nor wish the tender touch of your caress.

My mirror without your love starts to age—

My pen in vain begins to fill blank page.

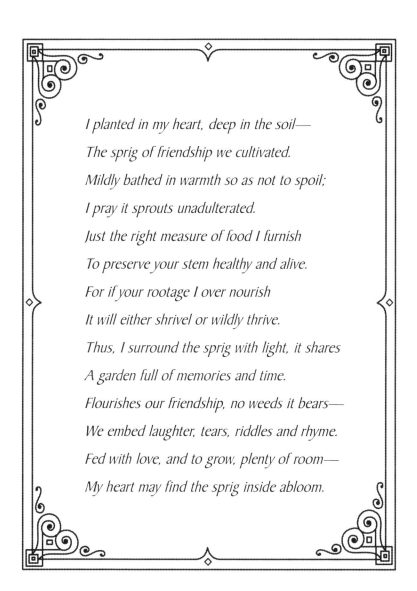

*I planted in my heart, deep in the soil—*

*The sprig of friendship we cultivated.*

*Mildly bathed in warmth so as not to spoil;*

*I pray it sprouts unadulterated.*

*Just the right measure of food I furnish*

*To preserve your stem healthy and alive.*

*For if your rootage I over nourish*

*It will either shrivel or wildly thrive.*

*Thus, I surround the sprig with light, it shares*

*A garden full of memories and time.*

*Flourishes our friendship, no weeds it bears—*

*We embed laughter, tears, riddles and rhyme.*

*Fed with love, and to grow, plenty of room—*

*My heart may find the sprig inside abloom.*

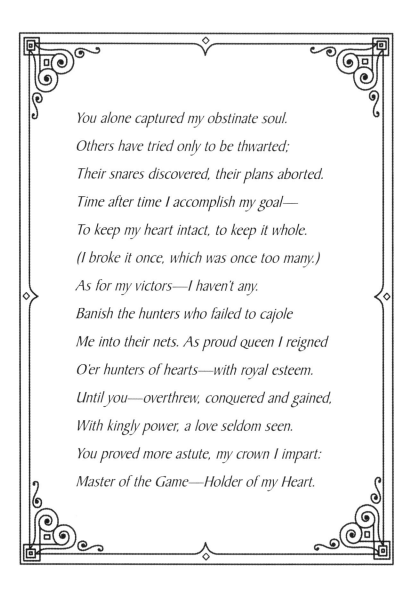

*You alone captured my obstinate soul.*

*Others have tried only to be thwarted;*

*Their snares discovered, their plans aborted.*

*Time after time I accomplish my goal—*

*To keep my heart intact, to keep it whole.*

*(I broke it once, which was once too many.)*

*As for my victors—I haven't any.*

*Banish the hunters who failed to cajole*

*Me into their nets. As proud Queen I reigned*

*O'er hunters of hearts—with royal esteem.*

*Until you—overthrew, conquered and gained,*

*With kingly power, a love seldom seen.*

*You proved more astute, my crown I impart:*

*Master of the Game—Holder of my Heart.*

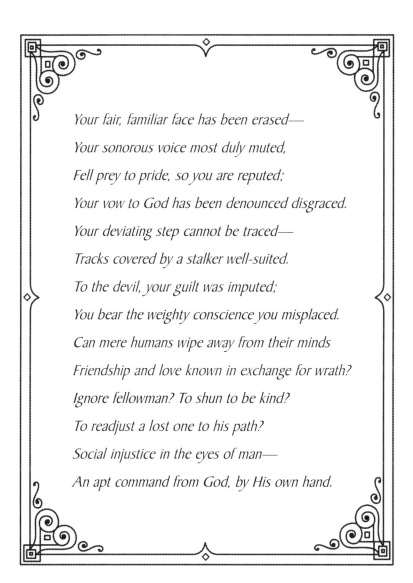

*Your fair, familiar face has been erased—*

*Your sonorous voice most duly muted,*

*Fell prey to pride, so you are reputed;*

*Your vow to God has been denounced disgraced.*

*Your deviating step cannot be traced—*

*Tracks covered by a stalker well-suited.*

*To the devil, your guilt was imputed;*

*You bear the weighty conscience you misplaced.*

*Can mere humans wipe away from their minds*

*Friendship and love known in exchange for wrath?*

*Ignore fellowman? To shun to be kind?*

*To readjust a lost one to his path?*

*Social injustice in the eyes of man—*

*An apt command from God, by His own hand.*

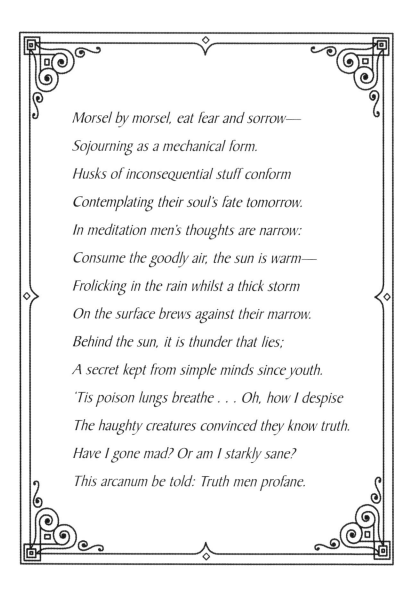

Morsel by morsel, eat fear and sorrow—

Sojourning as a mechanical form.

Husks of inconsequential stuff conform

Contemplating their soul's fate tomorrow.

In meditation men's thoughts are narrow:

Consume the goodly air, the sun is warm—

Frolicking in the rain whilst a thick storm

On the surface brews against their marrow.

Behind the sun, it is thunder that lies;

A secret kept from simple minds since youth.

'Tis poison lungs breathe . . . Oh, how I despise

The haughty creatures convinced they know truth.

Have I gone mad? Or am I starkly sane?

This arcanum be told: Truth men profane.

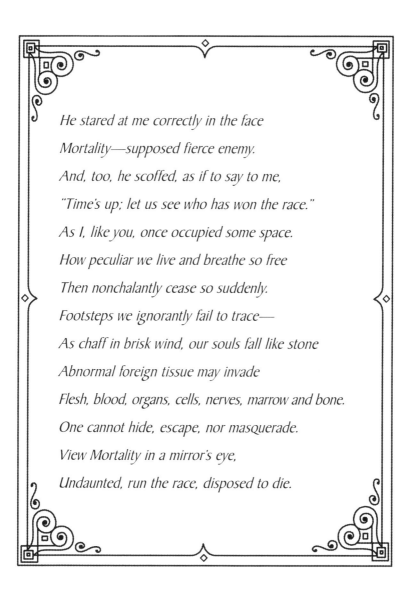

He stared at me correctly in the face

Mortality—supposed fierce enemy.

And, too, he scoffed, as if to say to me,

"Time's up; let us see who has won the race."

As I, like you, once occupied some space.

How peculiar we live and breathe so free

Then nonchalantly cease so suddenly.

Footsteps we ignorantly fail to trace—

As chaff in brisk wind, our souls fall like stone

Abnormal foreign tissue may invade

Flesh, blood, organs, cells, nerves, marrow and bone.

One cannot hide, escape, nor masquerade.

View Mortality in a mirror's eye,

Undaunted, run the race, disposed to die.

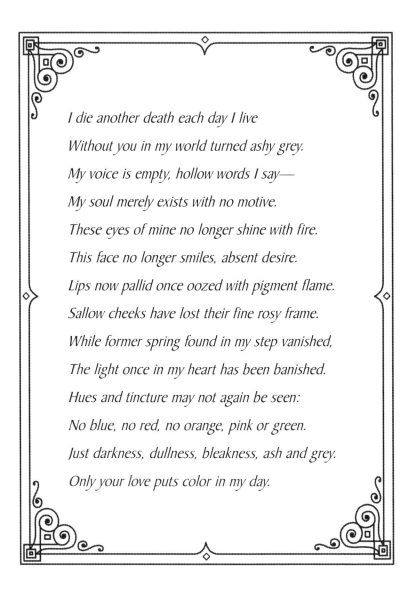

*I die another death each day I live*

*Without you in my world turned ashy grey.*

*My voice is empty, hollow words I say—*

*My soul merely exists with no motive.*

*These eyes of mine no longer shine with fire.*

*This face no longer smiles, absent desire.*

*Lips now pallid once oozed with pigment flame.*

*Sallow cheeks have lost their fine rosy frame.*

*While former spring found in my step vanished,*

*The light once in my heart has been banished.*

*Hues and tincture may not again be seen:*

*No blue, no red, no orange, pink or green.*

*Just darkness, dullness, bleakness, ash and grey.*

*Only your love puts color in my day.*

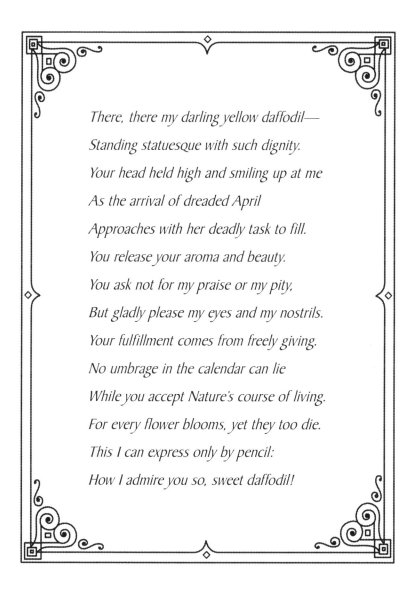

*There, there my darling yellow daffodil—*

*Standing statuesque with such dignity.*

*Your head held high and smiling up at me*

*As the arrival of dreaded April*

*Approaches with her deadly task to fill.*

*You release your aroma and beauty.*

*You ask not for my praise or my pity,*

*But gladly please my eyes and my nostrils.*

*Your fulfillment comes from freely giving.*

*No umbrage in the calendar can lie*

*While you accept Nature's course of living.*

*For every flower blooms, yet they too die.*

*This I can express only by pencil:*

*How I admire you so, sweet daffodil!*

Words fail me to convey my utter thrill
As my eyes fell upon the daffodil—
Deftly enchanting was its fragile form;
It left me in delight, aglow and warm.
My dear friends to bestow this precious gift
Gave me an ever-needed secret lift.
When skies are gloomy grey and days are blue
I'll gaze at it and think of both of you.
True brothers' gentle kindness, as it were—
Also gave me a smile, hence you'll concur:
That more than any shining star above
Is brightness brought forth from a gift of love.
On long and lonely nights, my mind I'll fill
With fond memories of my daffodil.

I heard my sister Sharon laugh today

A sound I had not heard in quite awhile

For years on her face all I saw was grey

A shadowed picture of a shadowed child

Had the girl once filled with spirit and life

Crawled into a dark cave inside her mind?

What was it in her past that brought her strife?

The answer lies beyond me not to find

One time she swelled with generosity

I knew her well, where had that sparrow flown

Who gave her heart and soul so willingly?

To her farewell, I weep yet not alone

Today I heard my sister Sharon laugh

She took her life and cut my own in half.

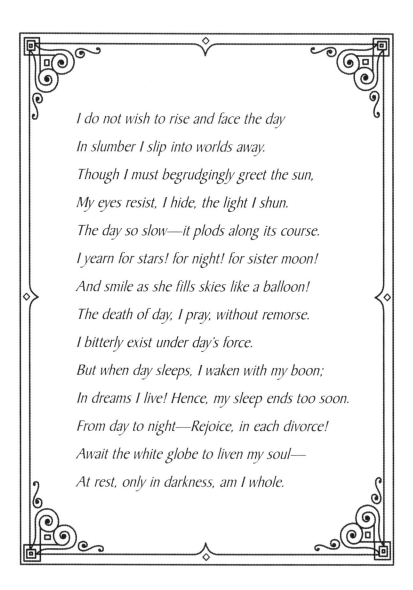

*I do not wish to rise and face the day*

*In slumber I slip into worlds away.*

*Though I must begrudgingly greet the sun,*

*My eyes resist, I hide, the light I shun.*

*The day so slow—it plods along its course.*

*I yearn for stars! for night! for sister moon!*

*And smile as she fills skies like a balloon!*

*The death of day, I pray, without remorse.*

*I bitterly exist under day's force.*

*But when day sleeps, I waken with my boon;*

*In dreams I live! Hence, my sleep ends too soon.*

*From day to night—Rejoice, in each divorce!*

*Await the white globe to liven my soul—*

*At rest, only in darkness, am I whole.*

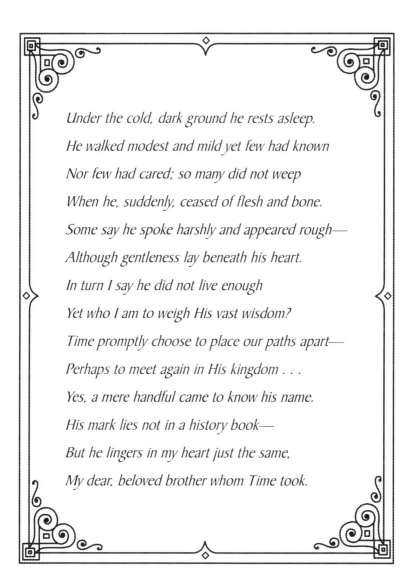

Under the cold, dark ground he rests asleep.

He walked modest and mild yet few had known

Nor few had cared; so many did not weep

When he, suddenly, ceased of flesh and bone.

Some say he spoke harshly and appeared rough—

Although gentleness lay beneath his heart.

In turn I say he did not live enough

Yet who I am to weigh His vast wisdom?

Time promptly choose to place our paths apart—

Perhaps to meet again in His kingdom . . .

Yes, a mere handful came to know his name.

His mark lies not in a history book—

But he lingers in my heart just the same,

My dear, beloved brother whom Time took.

In her still eyes emotions carousel;

To meet her once is, yes, to know her well.

Beauty within is evident without—

To all that is righteous, she is devout.

A taker of none—a giver of self

Bygone dreams of old, she stores on a shelf.

A lover of all—a giver of life,

She epitomizes mother and wife.

With vast modesty, offspring she did raise—

Takes no credit, to her Maker all praise.

A slice of her nature seen in each child;

The creative, the jester, and the mild.

Inspiring soft words encourage many

Of those so blessed to cross paths with Jenny.

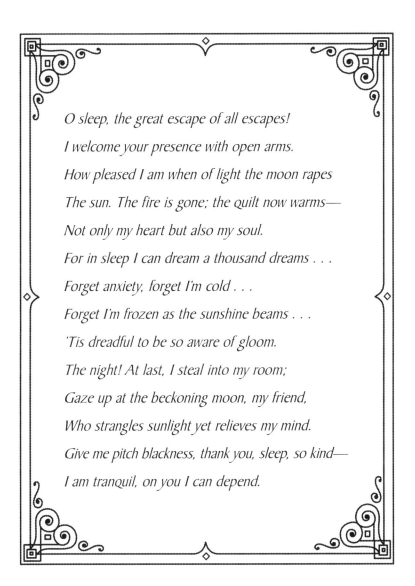

*O sleep, the great escape of all escapes!*

*I welcome your presence with open arms.*

*How pleased I am when of light the moon rapes*

*The sun. The fire is gone; the quilt now warms—*

*Not only my heart but also my soul.*

*For in sleep I can dream a thousand dreams . . .*

*Forget anxiety, forget I'm cold . . .*

*Forget I'm frozen as the sunshine beams . . .*

*'Tis dreadful to be so aware of gloom.*

*The night! At last, I steal into my room;*

*Gaze up at the beckoning moon, my friend,*

*Who strangles sunlight yet relieves my mind.*

*Give me pitch blackness, thank you, sleep, so kind—*

*I am tranquil, on you I can depend.*

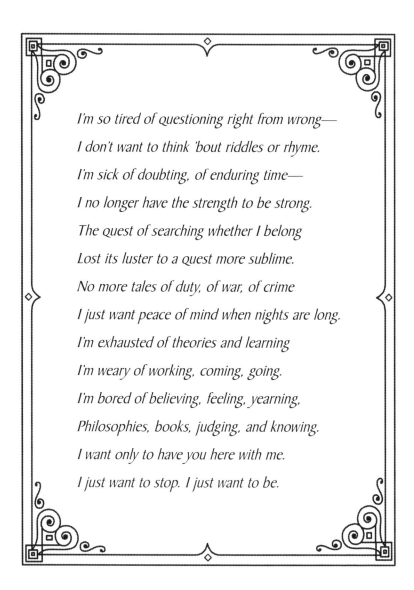

I'm so tired of questioning right from wrong—
I don't want to think 'bout riddles or rhyme.
I'm sick of doubting, of enduring time—
I no longer have the strength to be strong.
The quest of searching whether I belong
Lost its luster to a quest more sublime.
No more tales of duty, of war, of crime
I just want peace of mind when nights are long.
I'm exhausted of theories and learning
I'm weary of working, coming, going.
I'm bored of believing, feeling, yearning,
Philosophies, books, judging, and knowing.
I want only to have you here with me.
I just want to stop. I just want to be.

Despite my pride, against my will I bend

For words spill from my pen begrudgingly.

The medicine which I eat fervently.

You are not worth the ink I must expend

I comfort my soul, my heart to defend.

To see your scarless escape disgusts me.

As you saunter in so nonchalantly,

On my implements, I dryly depend.

I'm sickened with each sentence completed—

Rhythmically pour onto paper my grief

For it proves your heart has mine defeated.

Verse gives my heart only abstract relief

These words aren't for the cavalier and vain—

But for my sake, dignity to regain.

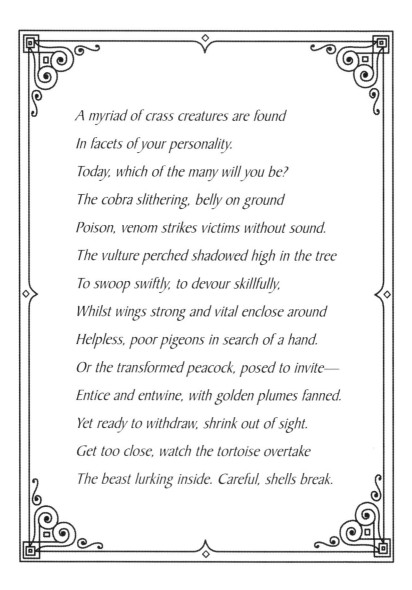

*A myriad of crass creatures are found*
*In facets of your personality.*
*Today, which of the many will you be?*
*The cobra slithering, belly on ground*
*Poison, venom strikes victims without sound.*
*The vulture perched shadowed high in the tree*
*To swoop swiftly, to devour skillfully,*
*Whilst wings strong and vital enclose around*
*Helpless, poor pigeons in search of a hand.*
*Or the transformed peacock, posed to invite—*
*Entice and entwine, with golden plumes fanned.*
*Yet ready to withdraw, shrink out of sight.*
*Get too close, watch the tortoise overtake*
*The beast lurking inside. Careful, shells break.*

I've had my fill of the Joker of Love

His tricks I can dodge no longer nor run

Away from his charm, no more is love fun.

This game is such drivel, beckoned above—

Freedom from his crafty, well-thought out pranks.

My eyes burn with tears shed from his teases,

Mockingly clowns with hearts as he pleases.

For his cruel antics, he'll receive no thanks.

Could he think his jesting is amusing?

Laugh at the contest I am well losing?

He's in cahoots with the devil of ole'—

A union I find uncannily droll.

I concede to the joust, forgo the duel,

You win, I give up—but who is the fool?

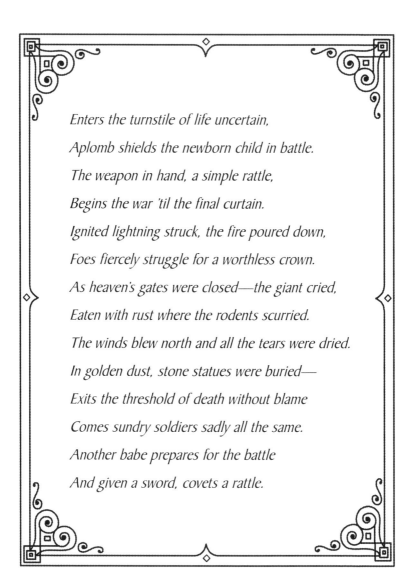

Enters the turnstile of life uncertain,

Aplomb shields the newborn child in battle.

The weapon in hand, a simple rattle,

Begins the war 'til the final curtain.

Ignited lightning struck, the fire poured down,

Foes fiercely struggle for a worthless crown.

As heaven's gates were closed—the giant cried,

Eaten with rust where the rodents scurried.

The winds blew north and all the tears were dried.

In golden dust, stone statues were buried—

Exits the threshold of death without blame

Comes sundry soldiers sadly all the same.

Another babe prepares for the battle

And given a sword, covets a rattle.

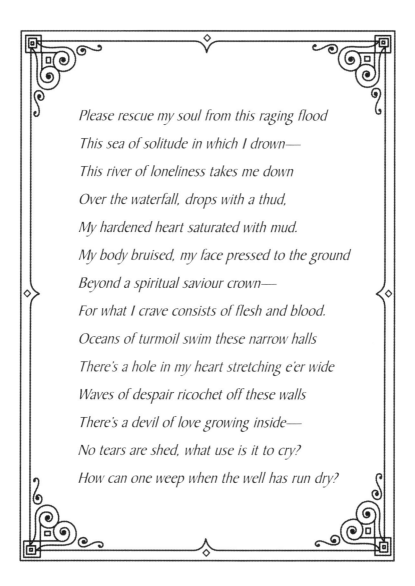

Please rescue my soul from this raging flood

This sea of solitude in which I drown—

This river of loneliness takes me down

Over the waterfall, drops with a thud,

My hardened heart saturated with mud.

My body bruised, my face pressed to the ground

Beyond a spiritual saviour crown—

For what I crave consists of flesh and blood.

Oceans of turmoil swim these narrow halls

There's a hole in my heart stretching e'er wide

Waves of despair ricochet off these walls

There's a devil of love growing inside—

No tears are shed, what use is it to cry?

How can one weep when the well has run dry?

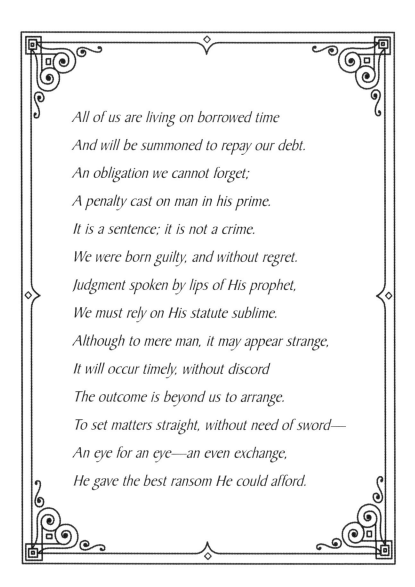

All of us are living on borrowed time

And will be summoned to repay our debt.

An obligation we cannot forget;

A penalty cast on man in his prime.

It is a sentence; it is not a crime.

We were born guilty, and without regret.

Judgment spoken by lips of His prophet,

We must rely on His statute sublime.

Although to mere man, it may appear strange,

It will occur timely, without discord

The outcome is beyond us to arrange.

To set matters straight, without need of sword—

An eye for an eye—an even exchange,

He gave the best ransom He could afford.

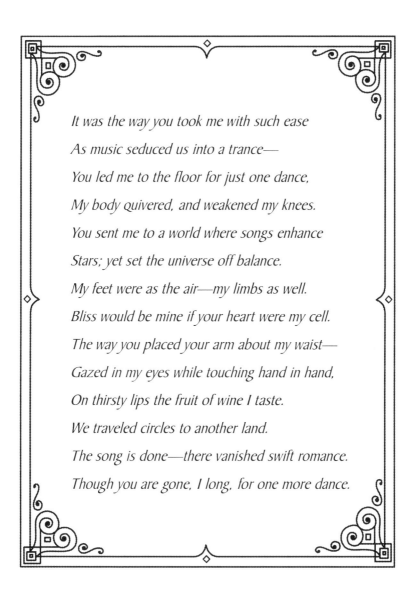

*It was the way you took me with such ease*

*As music seduced us into a trance—*

*You led me to the floor for just one dance,*

*My body quivered, and weakened my knees.*

*You sent me to a world where songs enhance*

*Stars; yet set the universe off balance.*

*My feet were as the air—my limbs as well.*

*Bliss would be mine if your heart were my cell.*

*The way you placed your arm about my waist—*

*Gazed in my eyes while touching hand in hand,*

*On thirsty lips the fruit of wine I taste.*

*We traveled circles to another land.*

*The song is done—there vanished swift romance.*

*Though you are gone, I long, for one more dance.*

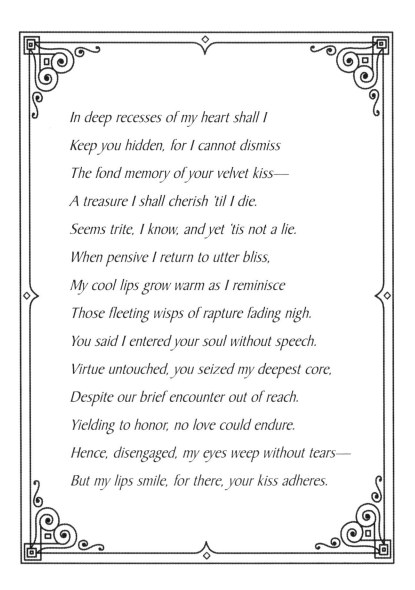

*In deep recesses of my heart shall I*

*Keep you hidden, for I cannot dismiss*

*The fond memory of your velvet kiss—*

*A treasure I shall cherish 'til I die.*

*Seems trite, I know, and yet 'tis not a lie.*

*When pensive I return to utter bliss,*

*My cool lips grow warm as I reminisce*

*Those fleeting wisps of rapture fading nigh.*

*You said I entered your soul without speech.*

*Virtue untouched, you seized my deepest core,*

*Despite our brief encounter out of reach.*

*Yielding to honor, no love could endure.*

*Hence, disengaged, my eyes weep without tears—*

*But my lips smile, for there, your kiss adheres.*

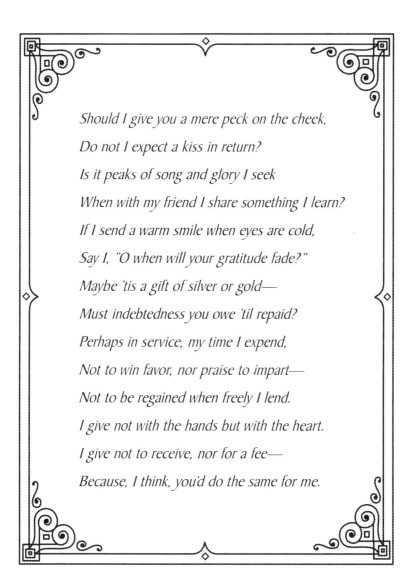

Should I give you a mere peck on the cheek,

Do not I expect a kiss in return?

Is it peaks of song and glory I seek

When with my friend I share something I learn?

If I send a warm smile when eyes are cold,

Say I, "O when will your gratitude fade?"

Maybe 'tis a gift of silver or gold—

Must indebtedness you owe 'til repaid?

Perhaps in service, my time I expend,

Not to win favor, nor praise to impart—

Not to be regained when freely I lend.

I give not with the hands but with the heart.

I give not to receive, nor for a fee—

Because, I think, you'd do the same for me.

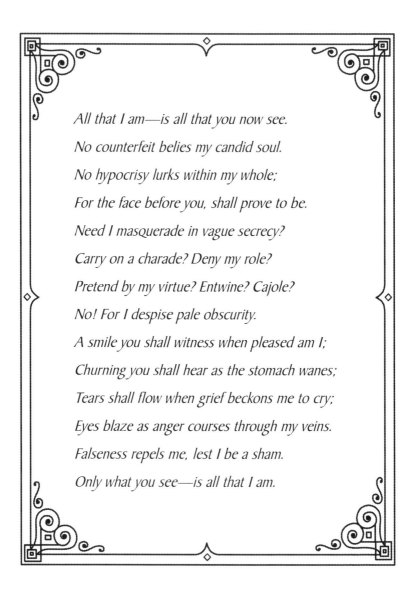

All that I am—is all that you now see.

No counterfeit belies my candid soul.

No hypocrisy lurks within my whole;

For the face before you, shall prove to be.

Need I masquerade in vague secrecy?

Carry on a charade? Deny my role?

Pretend by my virtue? Entwine? Cajole?

No! For I despise pale obscurity.

A smile you shall witness when pleased am I;

Churning you shall hear as the stomach wanes;

Tears shall flow when grief beckons me to cry;

Eyes blaze as anger courses through my veins.

Falseness repels me, lest I be a sham.

Only what you see—is all that I am.

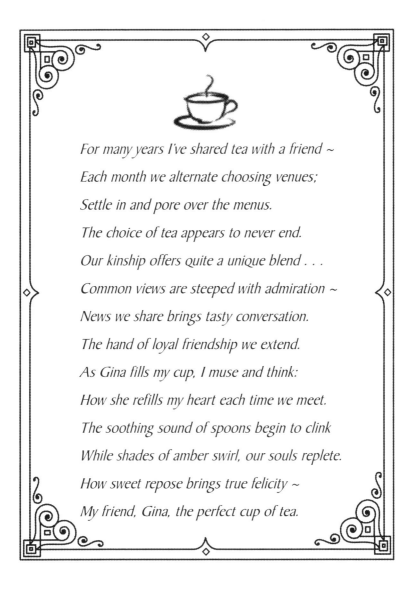

For many years I've shared tea with a friend ~

Each month we alternate choosing venues;

Settle in and pore over the menus.

The choice of tea appears to never end.

Our kinship offers quite a unique blend . . .

Common views are steeped with admiration ~

News we share brings tasty conversation.

The hand of loyal friendship we extend.

As Gina fills my cup, I muse and think:

How she refills my heart each time we meet.

The soothing sound of spoons begin to clink

While shades of amber swirl, our souls replete.

How sweet repose brings true felicity ~

My friend, Gina, the perfect cup of tea.

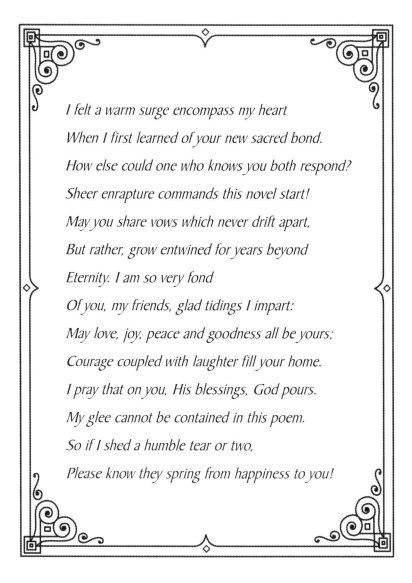

*I felt a warm surge encompass my heart*

*When I first learned of your new sacred bond.*

*How else could one who knows you both respond?*

*Sheer enrapture commands this novel start!*

*May you share vows which never drift apart,*

*But rather, grow entwined for years beyond*

*Eternity. I am so very fond*

*Of you, my friends, glad tidings I impart:*

*May love, joy, peace and goodness all be yours;*

*Courage coupled with laughter fill your home.*

*I pray that on you, His blessings, God pours.*

*My glee cannot be contained in this poem.*

*So if I shed a humble tear or two,*

*Please know they spring from happiness to you!*

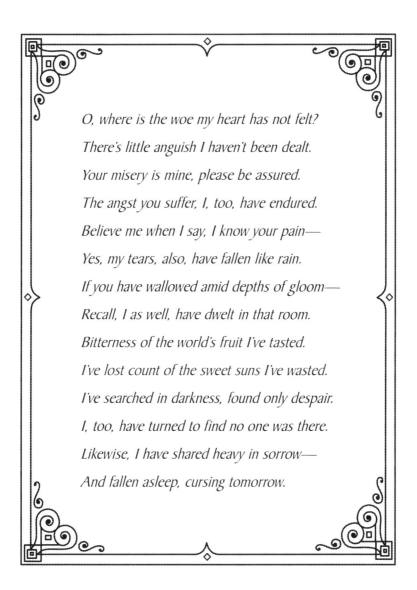

*O, where is the woe my heart has not felt?*

*There's little anguish I haven't been dealt.*

*Your misery is mine, please be assured.*

*The angst you suffer, I, too, have endured.*

*Believe me when I say, I know your pain—*

*Yes, my tears, also, have fallen like rain.*

*If you have wallowed amid depths of gloom—*

*Recall, I as well, have dwelt in that room.*

*Bitterness of the world's fruit I've tasted.*

*I've lost count of the sweet suns I've wasted.*

*I've searched in darkness, found only despair.*

*I, too, have turned to find no one was there.*

*Likewise, I have shared heavy in sorrow—*

*And fallen asleep, cursing tomorrow.*

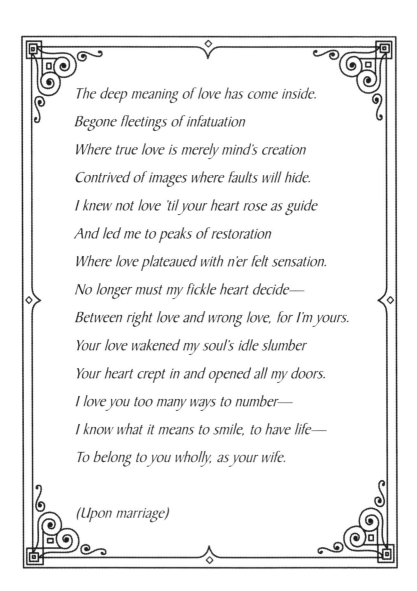

*The deep meaning of love has come inside.*

*Begone fleetings of infatuation*

*Where true love is merely mind's creation*

*Contrived of images where faults will hide.*

*I knew not love 'til your heart rose as guide*

*And led me to peaks of restoration*

*Where love plateaued with n'er felt sensation.*

*No longer must my fickle heart decide—*

*Between right love and wrong love, for I'm yours.*

*Your love wakened my soul's idle slumber*

*Your heart crept in and opened all my doors.*

*I love you too many ways to number—*

*I know what it means to smile, to have life—*

*To belong to you wholly, as your wife.*

*(Upon marriage)*

Even a god is allowed one mistake
No matter how trifling, albeit grave.
And oh, what an error did Cupid make
When to me, your heart, he faultily gave.
There must have been a bend in his sweet bow—
Perchance, in haste, he seized the wrong quiver?
Maybe he misaimed his love-dipped arrow?
For, when it pierced my heart, a cold shiver
Crept up my spine and stood my hair on end!
Yes, love, it's true, we both fancied to find.
On this Cherub's target I can't depend
Because you weren't quite what I had in mind.
What's done is done—no use to fret or cry;
Perhaps Cupid knows me better than I.

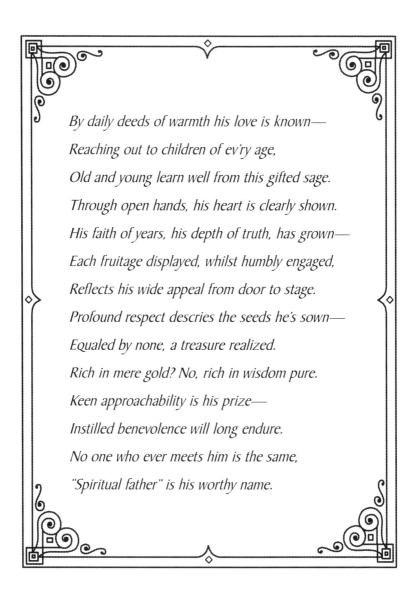

By daily deeds of warmth his love is known—

Reaching out to children of ev'ry age,

Old and young learn well from this gifted sage.

Through open hands, his heart is clearly shown.

His faith of years, his depth of truth, has grown—

Each fruitage displayed, whilst humbly engaged,

Reflects his wide appeal from door to stage.

Profound respect descries the seeds he's sown—

Equaled by none, a treasure realized.

Rich in mere gold? No, rich in wisdom pure.

Keen approachability is his prize—

Instilled benevolence will long endure.

No one who ever meets him is the same,

"Spiritual father" is his worthy name.

Always counting the time and not the cost

Of friendship rich and long, yet friendship lost.

Through your turnstile, fresh new faces appear—

Hypocrisy here, disenchantment there;

Acquaintances used as consolation

By you. Whereas, I know isolation.

Filling the empty hours, you bespeak

Kind duplicity, purportedly meek.

Feigning friendship with those merely strangers

While I alone am wise to your dangers.

Happy-go-lucky? Carefree? Here's how so . . .

Cares not of the miseries you bestow.

Am I to function with this known sorrow?

And embrace a Judas kiss tomorrow?

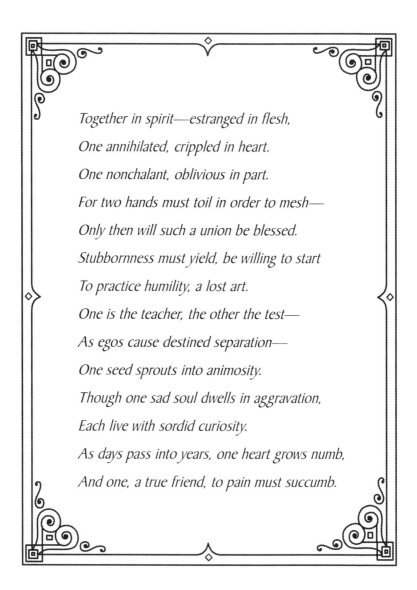

Together in spirit—estranged in flesh,

One annihilated, crippled in heart.

One nonchalant, oblivious in part.

For two hands must toil in order to mesh—

Only then will such a union be blessed.

Stubbornness must yield, be willing to start

To practice humility, a lost art.

One is the teacher, the other the test—

As egos cause destined separation—

One seed sprouts into animosity.

Though one sad soul dwells in aggravation,

Each live with sordid curiosity.

As days pass into years, one heart grows numb,

And one, a true friend, to pain must succumb.

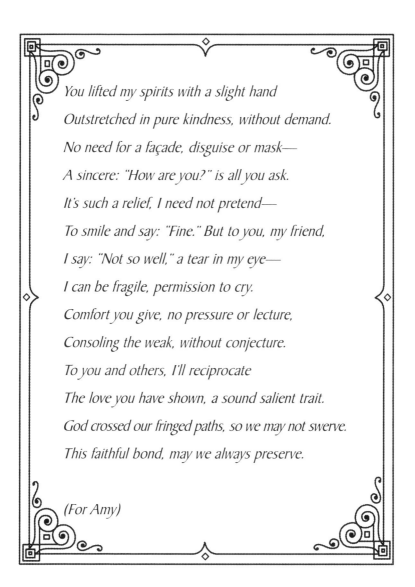

*You lifted my spirits with a slight hand*

*Outstretched in pure kindness, without demand.*

*No need for a façade, disguise or mask—*

*A sincere: "How are you?" is all you ask.*

*It's such a relief, I need not pretend—*

*To smile and say: "Fine." But to you, my friend,*

*I say: "Not so well," a tear in my eye—*

*I can be fragile, permission to cry.*

*Comfort you give, no pressure or lecture,*

*Consoling the weak, without conjecture.*

*To you and others, I'll reciprocate*

*The love you have shown, a sound salient trait.*

*God crossed our fringed paths, so we may not swerve.*

*This faithful bond, may we always preserve.*

*(For Amy)*

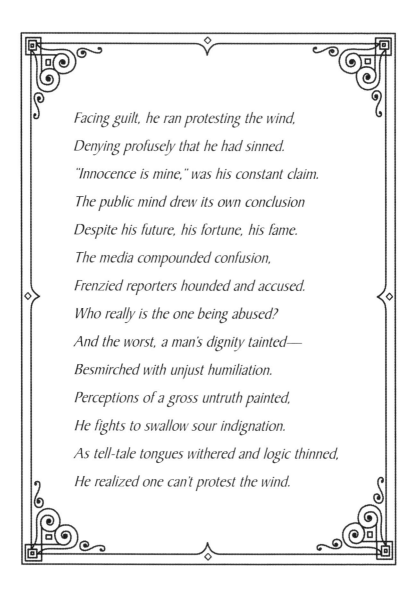

Facing guilt, he ran protesting the wind,

Denying profusely that he had sinned.

"Innocence is mine," was his constant claim.

The public mind drew its own conclusion

Despite his future, his fortune, his fame.

The media compounded confusion,

Frenzied reporters hounded and accused.

Who really is the one being abused?

And the worst, a man's dignity tainted—

Besmirched with unjust humiliation.

Perceptions of a gross untruth painted,

He fights to swallow sour indignation.

As tell-tale tongues withered and logic thinned,

He realized one can't protest the wind.

The scarecrow hangs on a nail on a pole.

Where a heart should be, there is a huge hole.

Without much substance, she sways in the breeze.

She's stuffed with emptiness, like a disease.

Poor old scarecrow stands alone in the field—

To desires and whims, she's forced to yield.

With limbs of straw, she's lost all her feeling,

The farmer sends her hay-filled head reeling.

He barks and shouts when crows pluck her sweet corn,

He put her there only to mock and scorn.

The violent winds and rains, she must weather.

Yet still she sings like a lilting feather.

The stake on her back compels her to stay.

I wish I could take the scarecrow away.

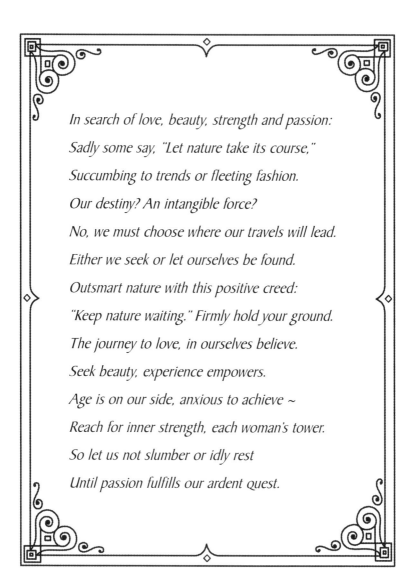

*In search of love, beauty, strength and passion:*

*Sadly some say, "Let nature take its course,"*

*Succumbing to trends or fleeting fashion.*

*Our destiny? An intangible force?*

*No, we must choose where our travels will lead.*

*Either we seek or let ourselves be found.*

*Outsmart nature with this positive creed:*

*"Keep nature waiting." Firmly hold your ground.*

*The journey to love, in ourselves believe.*

*Seek beauty, experience empowers.*

*Age is on our side, anxious to achieve ~*

*Reach for inner strength, each woman's tower.*

*So let us not slumber or idly rest*

*Until passion fulfills our ardent quest.*

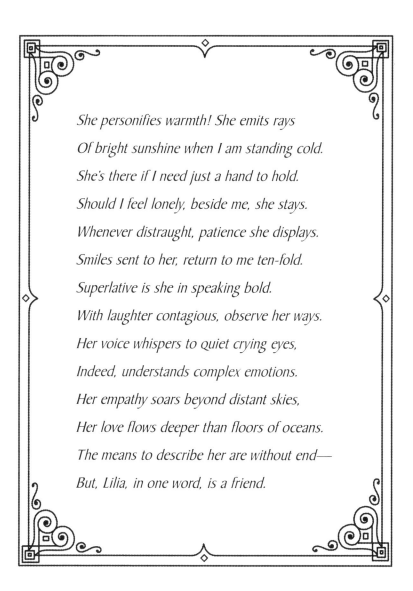

*She personifies warmth! She emits rays*

*Of bright sunshine when I am standing cold.*

*She's there if I need just a hand to hold.*

*Should I feel lonely, beside me, she stays.*

*Whenever distraught, patience she displays.*

*Smiles sent to her, return to me ten-fold.*

*Superlative is she in speaking bold.*

*With laughter contagious, observe her ways.*

*Her voice whispers to quiet crying eyes,*

*Indeed, understands complex emotions.*

*Her empathy soars beyond distant skies,*

*Her love flows deeper than floors of oceans.*

*The means to describe her are without end—*

*But, Lilia, in one word, is a friend.*

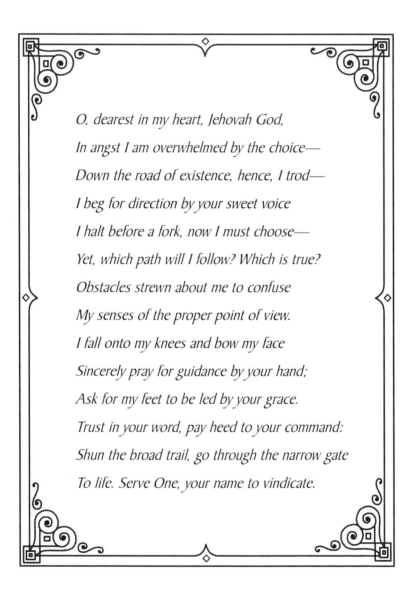

O, dearest in my heart, Jehovah God,
In angst I am overwhelmed by the choice—
Down the road of existence, hence, I trod—
I beg for direction by your sweet voice
I halt before a fork, now I must choose—
Yet, which path will I follow? Which is true?
Obstacles strewn about me to confuse
My senses of the proper point of view.
I fall onto my knees and bow my face
Sincerely pray for guidance by your hand;
Ask for my feet to be led by your grace.
Trust in your word, pay heed to your command:
Shun the broad trail, go through the narrow gate
To life. Serve One, your name to vindicate.

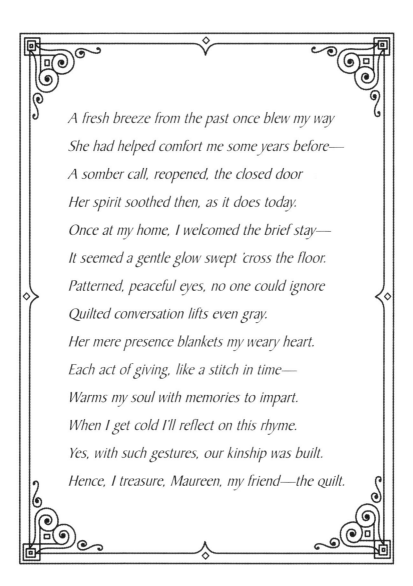

A fresh breeze from the past once blew my way

She had helped comfort me some years before—

A somber call, reopened, the closed door

Her spirit soothed then, as it does today.

Once at my home, I welcomed the brief stay—

It seemed a gentle glow swept 'cross the floor.

Patterned, peaceful eyes, no one could ignore

Quilted conversation lifts even gray.

Her mere presence blankets my weary heart.

Each act of giving, like a stitch in time—

Warms my soul with memories to impart.

When I get cold I'll reflect on this rhyme.

Yes, with such gestures, our kinship was built.

Hence, I treasure, Maureen, my friend—the quilt.

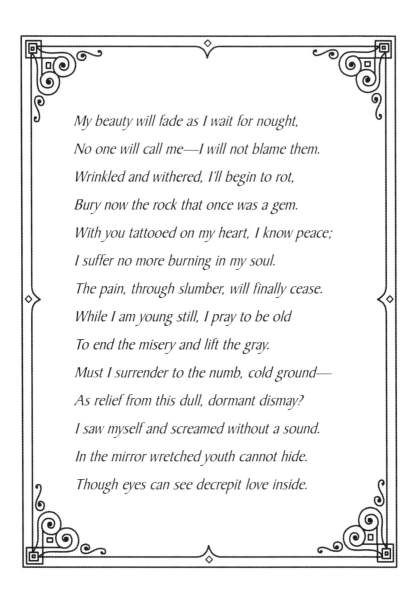

*My beauty will fade as I wait for nought,*

*No one will call me—I will not blame them.*

*Wrinkled and withered, I'll begin to rot,*

*Bury now the rock that once was a gem.*

*With you tattooed on my heart, I know peace;*

*I suffer no more burning in my soul.*

*The pain, through slumber, will finally cease.*

*While I am young still, I pray to be old*

*To end the misery and lift the gray.*

*Must I surrender to the numb, cold ground—*

*As relief from this dull, dormant dismay?*

*I saw myself and screamed without a sound.*

*In the mirror wretched youth cannot hide.*

*Though eyes can see decrepit love inside.*

*The fog lifts subtly like a virgin's veil;*

*Anticipation envelopes my mind.*

*Many months have passed with clouds ever pale—*

*In my head and my heart they have aligned.*

*My smile has been lost, my laughter declined.*

*Now, like a torrent, I feel them surging.*

*A break in the clouds—my soul is urging*

*My will to leave trepidation behind.*

*Come out of the mist, come into the light.*

*Expose the shadow that hides like a child.*

*Embrace the sun, bid the tired moon goodnight.*

*Fear not the unknown or the fog beguiled.*

*The curtains pulled back, rays dance on the floor—*

*The fog dissipates to hound me no more.*

My stagnant heart leapt up with the bright sun

As you wrapped me close in your forceful wings.

Rejoice in song! O, how my real love sings.

Could it be so our love has just begun?

Souls once two have since welded into one?

Erase the clouds and rain that Nature brings

As the harp of love plays with our heartstrings.

Never shall our fastened souls grow undone—

Half of us will not begin to live, for

As you draw shallow breath, you breathe for me.

Rich in mere gold? No, rich in mirth so pure.

Vanish the grey from our hearts—set us free.

Emit the light which shines forevermore

Yet with the subtle lamp of ecstasy.

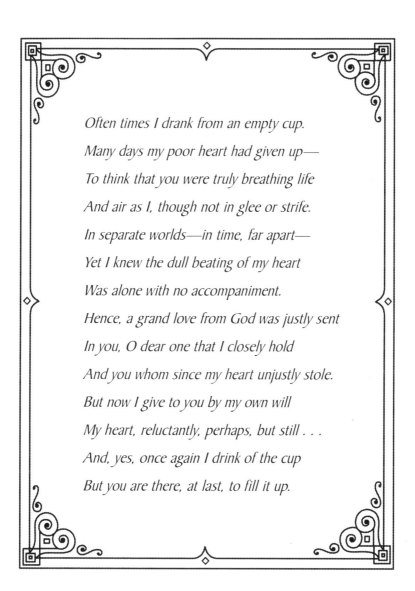

Often times I drank from an empty cup.

Many days my poor heart had given up—

To think that you were truly breathing life

And air as I, though not in glee or strife.

In separate worlds—in time, far apart—

Yet I knew the dull beating of my heart

Was alone with no accompaniment.

Hence, a grand love from God was justly sent

In you, O dear one that I closely hold

And you whom since my heart unjustly stole.

But now I give to you by my own will

My heart, reluctantly, perhaps, but still . . .

And, yes, once again I drink of the cup

But you are there, at last, to fill it up.

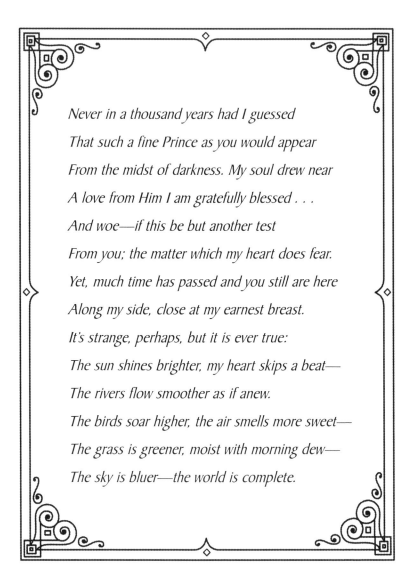

*Never in a thousand years had I guessed*
*That such a fine Prince as you would appear*
*From the midst of darkness. My soul drew near*
*A love from Him I am gratefully blessed . . .*
*And woe—if this be but another test*
*From you; the matter which my heart does fear.*
*Yet, much time has passed and you still are here*
*Along my side, close at my earnest breast.*
*It's strange, perhaps, but it is ever true:*
*The sun shines brighter, my heart skips a beat—*
*The rivers flow smoother as if anew.*
*The birds soar higher, the air smells more sweet—*
*The grass is greener, moist with morning dew—*
*The sky is bluer—the world is complete.*

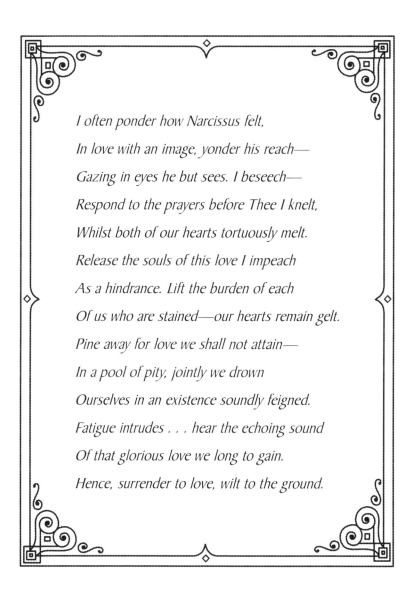

*I often ponder how Narcissus felt,*

*In love with an image, yonder his reach—*

*Gazing in eyes he but sees. I beseech—*

*Respond to the prayers before Thee I knelt,*

*Whilst both of our hearts tortuously melt.*

*Release the souls of this love I impeach*

*As a hindrance. Lift the burden of each*

*Of us who are stained—our hearts remain gelt.*

*Pine away for love we shall not attain—*

*In a pool of pity, jointly we drown*

*Ourselves in an existence soundly feigned.*

*Fatigue intrudes . . . hear the echoing sound*

*Of that glorious love we long to gain.*

*Hence, surrender to love, wilt to the ground.*

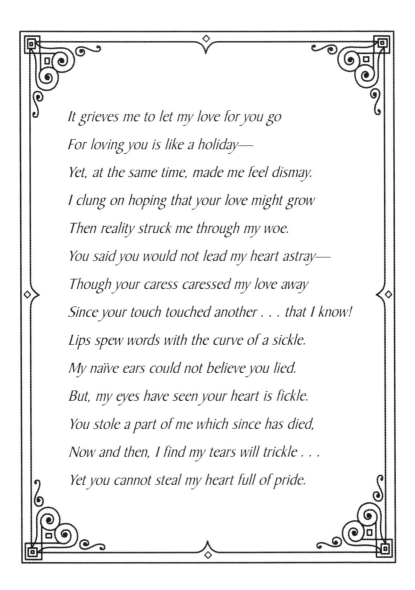

*It grieves me to let my love for you go*

*For loving you is like a holiday—*

*Yet, at the same time, made me feel dismay.*

*I clung on hoping that your love might grow*

*Then reality struck me through my woe.*

*You said you would not lead my heart astray—*

*Though your caress caressed my love away*

*Since your touch touched another . . . that I know!*

*Lips spew words with the curve of a sickle.*

*My naïve ears could not believe you lied.*

*But, my eyes have seen your heart is fickle.*

*You stole a part of me which since has died,*

*Now and then, I find my tears will trickle . . .*

*Yet you cannot steal my heart full of pride.*

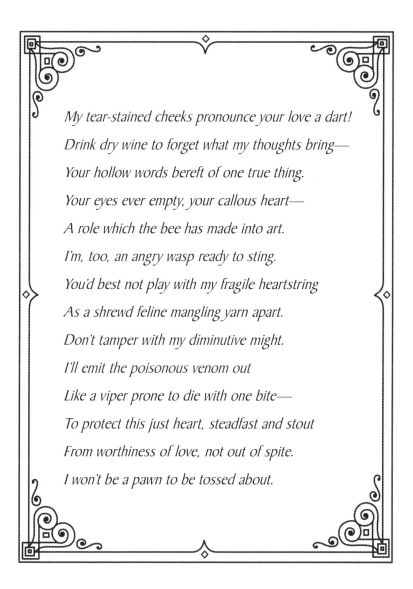

My tear-stained cheeks pronounce your love a dart!

Drink dry wine to forget what my thoughts bring—

Your hollow words bereft of one true thing.

Your eyes ever empty, your callous heart—

A role which the bee has made into art.

I'm, too, an angry wasp ready to sting.

You'd best not play with my fragile heartstring

As a shrewd feline mangling yarn apart.

Don't tamper with my diminutive might.

I'll emit the poisonous venom out

Like a viper prone to die with one bite—

To protect this just heart, steadfast and stout

From worthiness of love, not out of spite.

I won't be a pawn to be tossed about.

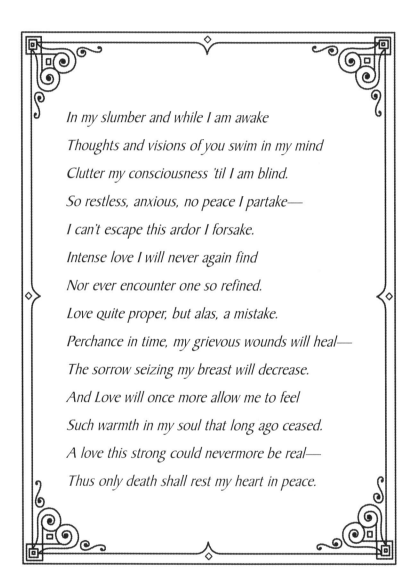

*In my slumber and while I am awake*

*Thoughts and visions of you swim in my mind*

*Clutter my consciousness 'til I am blind.*

*So restless, anxious, no peace I partake—*

*I can't escape this ardor I forsake.*

*Intense love I will never again find*

*Nor ever encounter one so refined.*

*Love quite proper, but alas, a mistake.*

*Perchance in time, my grievous wounds will heal—*

*The sorrow seizing my breast will decrease.*

*And Love will once more allow me to feel*

*Such warmth in my soul that long ago ceased.*

*A love this strong could nevermore be real—*

*Thus only death shall rest my heart in peace.*

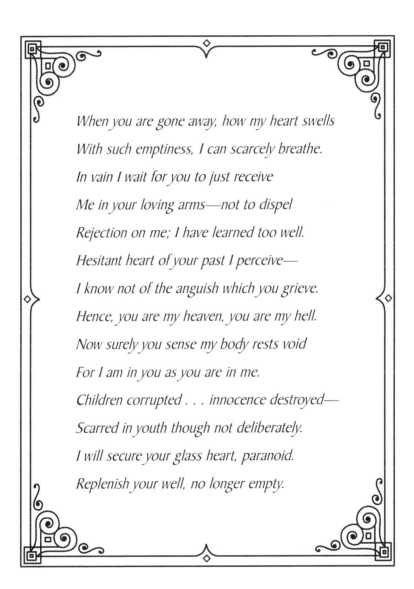

*When you are gone away, how my heart swells*

*With such emptiness, I can scarcely breathe.*

*In vain I wait for you to just receive*

*Me in your loving arms—not to dispel*

*Rejection on me; I have learned too well.*

*Hesitant heart of your past I perceive—*

*I know not of the anguish which you grieve.*

*Hence, you are my heaven, you are my hell.*

*Now surely you sense my body rests void*

*For I am in you as you are in me.*

*Children corrupted . . . innocence destroyed—*

*Scarred in youth though not deliberately.*

*I will secure your glass heart, paranoid.*

*Replenish your well, no longer empty.*

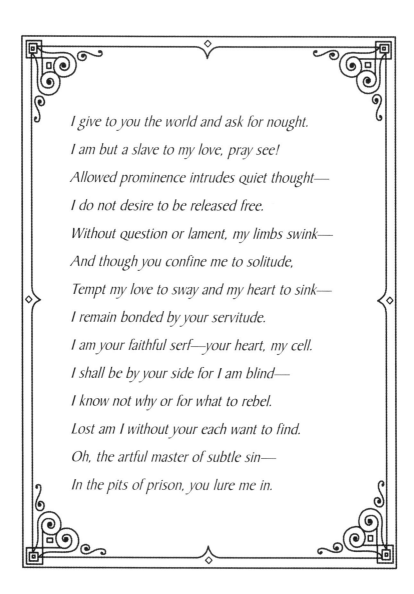

*I give to you the world and ask for nought.*

*I am but a slave to my love, pray see!*

*Allowed prominence intrudes quiet thought—*

*I do not desire to be released free.*

*Without question or lament, my limbs swink—*

*And though you confine me to solitude,*

*Tempt my love to sway and my heart to sink—*

*I remain bonded by your servitude.*

*I am your faithful serf—your heart, my cell.*

*I shall be by your side for I am blind—*

*I know not why or for what to rebel.*

*Lost am I without your each want to find.*

*Oh, the artful master of subtle sin—*

*In the pits of prison, you lure me in.*

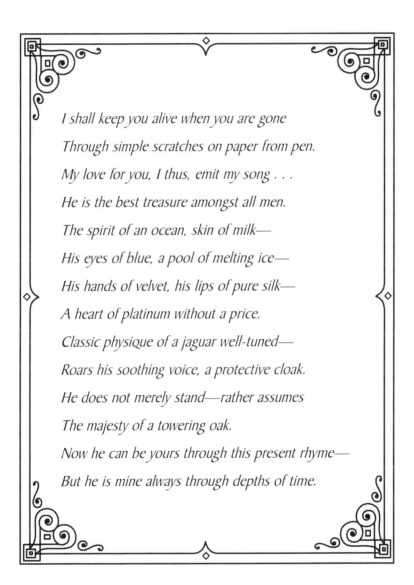

I shall keep you alive when you are gone

Through simple scratches on paper from pen.

My love for you, I thus, emit my song . . .

He is the best treasure amongst all men.

The spirit of an ocean, skin of milk—

His eyes of blue, a pool of melting ice—

His hands of velvet, his lips of pure silk—

A heart of platinum without a price.

Classic physique of a jaguar well-tuned—

Roars his soothing voice, a protective cloak.

He does not merely stand—rather assumes

The majesty of a towering oak.

Now he can be yours through this present rhyme—

But he is mine always through depths of time.

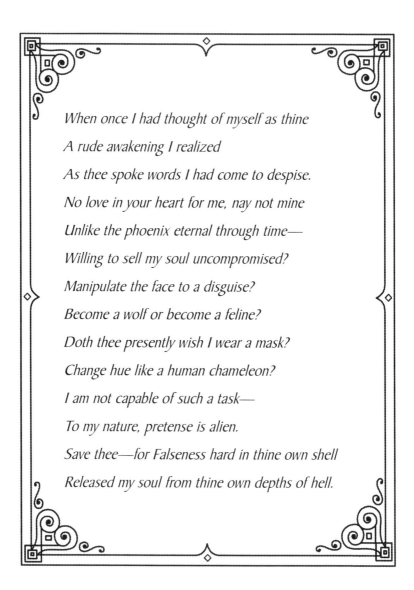

*When once I had thought of myself as thine*

*A rude awakening I realized*

*As thee spoke words I had come to despise.*

*No love in your heart for me, nay not mine*

*Unlike the phoenix eternal through time—*

*Willing to sell my soul uncompromised?*

*Manipulate the face to a disguise?*

*Become a wolf or become a feline?*

*Doth thee presently wish I wear a mask?*

*Change hue like a human chameleon?*

*I am not capable of such a task—*

*To my nature, pretense is alien.*

*Save thee—for Falseness hard in thine own shell*

*Released my soul from thine own depths of hell.*

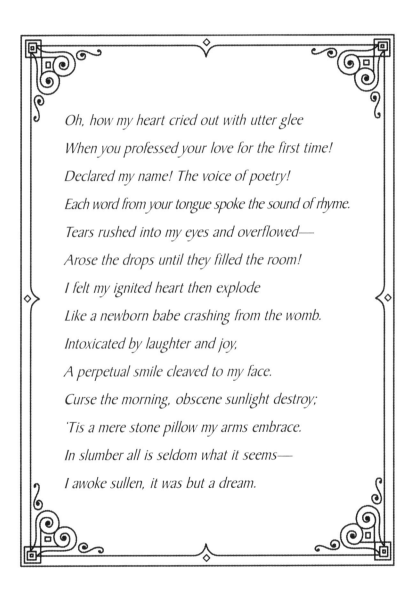

Oh, how my heart cried out with utter glee
When you professed your love for the first time!
Declared my name! The voice of poetry!
Each word from your tongue spoke the sound of rhyme.
Tears rushed into my eyes and overflowed—
Arose the drops until they filled the room!
I felt my ignited heart then explode
Like a newborn babe crashing from the womb.
Intoxicated by laughter and joy,
A perpetual smile cleaved to my face.
Curse the morning, obscene sunlight destroy;
'Tis a mere stone pillow my arms embrace.
In slumber all is seldom what it seems—
I awoke sullen, it was but a dream.

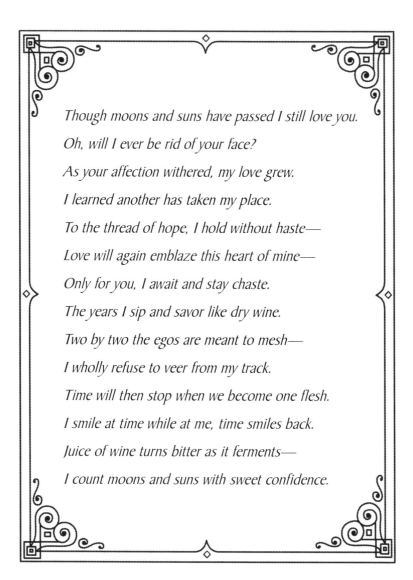

*Though moons and suns have passed I still love you.*

*Oh, will I ever be rid of your face?*

*As your affection withered, my love grew.*

*I learned another has taken my place.*

*To the thread of hope, I hold without haste—*

*Love will again emblaze this heart of mine—*

*Only for you, I await and stay chaste.*

*The years I sip and savor like dry wine.*

*Two by two the egos are meant to mesh—*

*I wholly refuse to veer from my track.*

*Time will then stop when we become one flesh.*

*I smile at time while at me, time smiles back.*

*Juice of wine turns bitter as it ferments—*

*I count moons and suns with sweet confidence.*

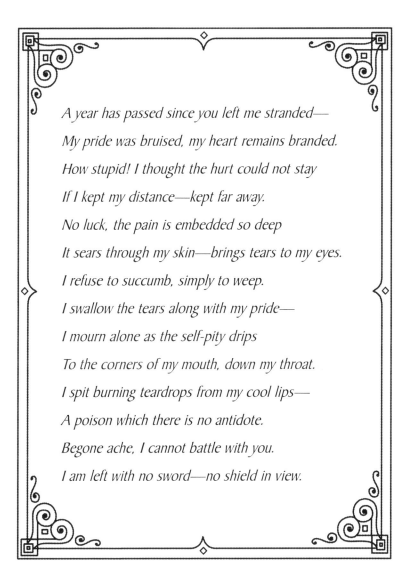

*A year has passed since you left me stranded—*

*My pride was bruised, my heart remains branded.*

*How stupid! I thought the hurt could not stay*

*If I kept my distance—kept far away.*

*No luck, the pain is embedded so deep*

*It sears through my skin—brings tears to my eyes.*

*I refuse to succumb, simply to weep.*

*I swallow the tears along with my pride—*

*I mourn alone as the self-pity drips*

*To the corners of my mouth, down my throat.*

*I spit burning teardrops from my cool lips—*

*A poison which there is no antidote.*

*Begone ache, I cannot battle with you.*

*I am left with no sword—no shield in view.*

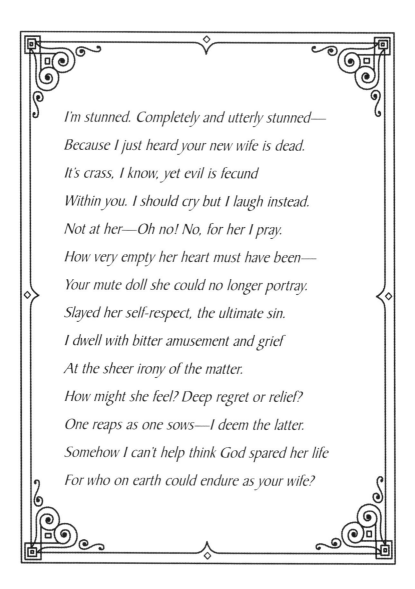

I'm stunned. Completely and utterly stunned—

Because I just heard your new wife is dead.

It's crass, I know, yet evil is fecund

Within you. I should cry but I laugh instead.

Not at her—Oh no! No, for her I pray.

How very empty her heart must have been—

Your mute doll she could no longer portray.

Slayed her self-respect, the ultimate sin.

I dwell with bitter amusement and grief

At the sheer irony of the matter.

How might she feel? Deep regret or relief?

One reaps as one sows—I deem the latter.

Somehow I can't help think God spared her life

For who on earth could endure as your wife?

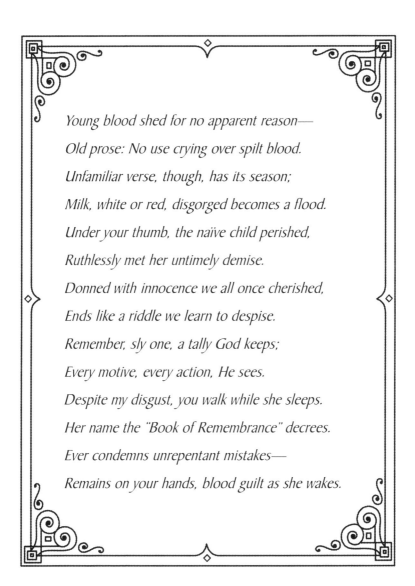

*Young blood shed for no apparent reason—*
*Old prose: No use crying over spilt blood.*
*Unfamiliar verse, though, has its season;*
*Milk, white or red, disgorged becomes a flood.*
*Under your thumb, the naïve child perished,*
*Ruthlessly met her untimely demise.*
*Donned with innocence we all once cherished,*
*Ends like a riddle we learn to despise.*
*Remember, sly one, a tally God keeps;*
*Every motive, every action, He sees.*
*Despite my disgust, you walk while she sleeps.*
*Her name the "Book of Remembrance" decrees.*
*Ever condemns unrepentant mistakes—*
*Remains on your hands, blood guilt as she wakes.*

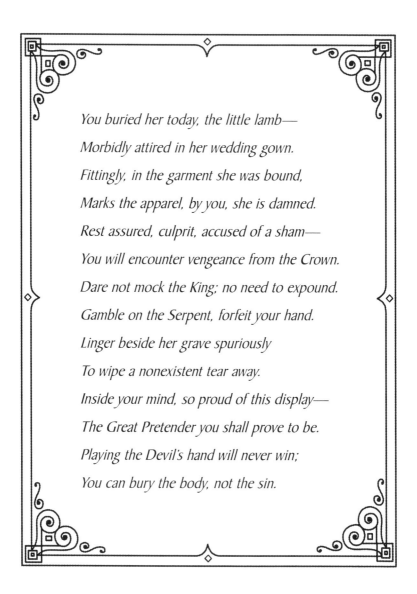

*You buried her today, the little lamb—*

*Morbidly attired in her wedding gown.*

*Fittingly, in the garment she was bound,*

*Marks the apparel, by you, she is damned.*

*Rest assured, culprit, accused of a sham—*

*You will encounter vengeance from the Crown.*

*Dare not mock the King; no need to expound.*

*Gamble on the Serpent, forfeit your hand.*

*Linger beside her grave spuriously*

*To wipe a nonexistent tear away.*

*Inside your mind, so proud of this display—*

*The Great Pretender you shall prove to be.*

*Playing the Devil's hand will never win;*

*You can bury the body, not the sin.*

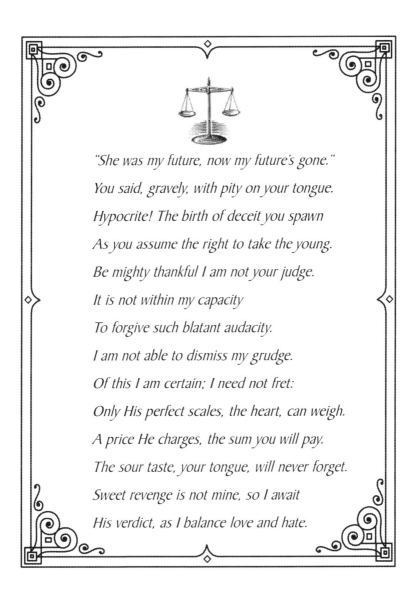

"She was my future, now my future's gone."

You said, gravely, with pity on your tongue.

Hypocrite! The birth of deceit you spawn

As you assume the right to take the young.

Be mighty thankful I am not your judge.

It is not within my capacity

To forgive such blatant audacity.

I am not able to dismiss my grudge.

Of this I am certain; I need not fret:

Only His perfect scales, the heart, can weigh.

A price He charges, the sum you will pay.

The sour taste, your tongue, will never forget.

Sweet revenge is not mine, so I await

His verdict, as I balance love and hate.

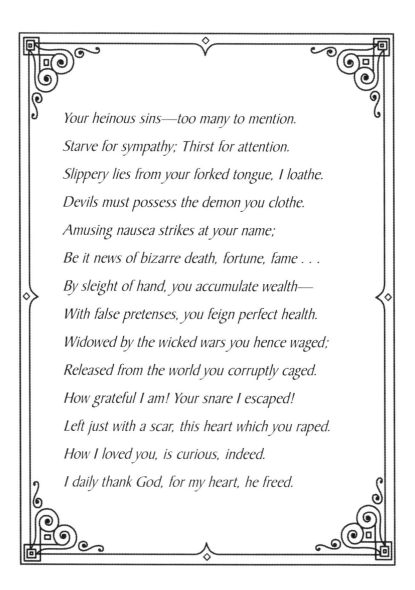

Your heinous sins—too many to mention.

Starve for sympathy; Thirst for attention.

Slippery lies from your forked tongue, I loathe.

Devils must possess the demon you clothe.

Amusing nausea strikes at your name;

Be it news of bizarre death, fortune, fame . . .

By sleight of hand, you accumulate wealth—

With false pretenses, you feign perfect health.

Widowed by the wicked wars you hence waged;

Released from the world you corruptly caged.

How grateful I am! Your snare I escaped!

Left just with a scar, this heart which you raped.

How I loved you, is curious, indeed.

I daily thank God, for my heart, he freed.

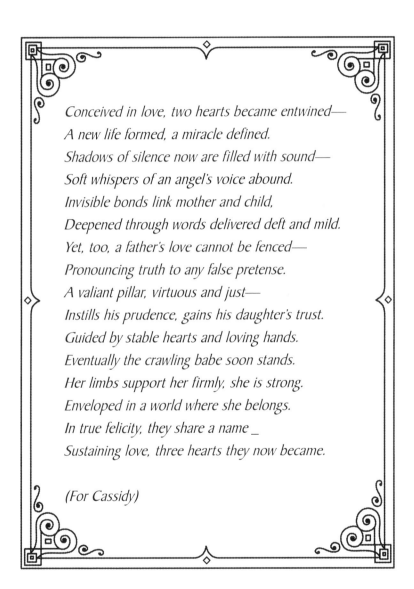

Conceived in love, two hearts became entwined—
A new life formed, a miracle defined.
Shadows of silence now are filled with sound—
Soft whispers of an angel's voice abound.
Invisible bonds link mother and child,
Deepened through words delivered deft and mild.
Yet, too, a father's love cannot be fenced—
Pronouncing truth to any false pretense.
A valiant pillar, virtuous and just—
Instills his prudence, gains his daughter's trust.
Guided by stable hearts and loving hands.
Eventually the crawling babe soon stands.
Her limbs support her firmly, she is strong.
Enveloped in a world where she belongs.
In true felicity, they share a name _
Sustaining love, three hearts they now became.

(For Cassidy)

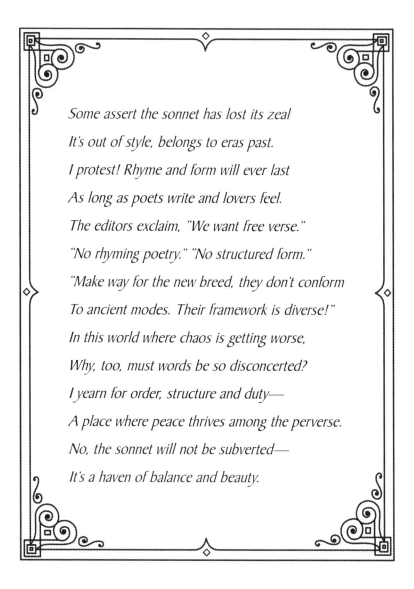

Some assert the sonnet has lost its zeal

It's out of style, belongs to eras past.

I protest! Rhyme and form will ever last

As long as poets write and lovers feel.

The editors exclaim, "We want free verse."

"No rhyming poetry." "No structured form."

"Make way for the new breed, they don't conform

To ancient modes. Their framework is diverse!"

In this world where chaos is getting worse,

Why, too, must words be so disconcerted?

I yearn for order, structure and duty—

A place where peace thrives among the perverse.

No, the sonnet will not be subverted—

It's a haven of balance and beauty.

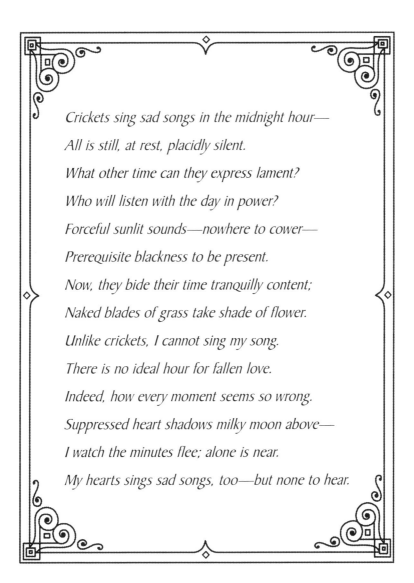

*Crickets sing sad songs in the midnight hour—*

*All is still, at rest, placidly silent.*

*What other time can they express lament?*

*Who will listen with the day in power?*

*Forceful sunlit sounds—nowhere to cower—*

*Prerequisite blackness to be present.*

*Now, they bide their time tranquilly content;*

*Naked blades of grass take shade of flower.*

*Unlike crickets, I cannot sing my song.*

*There is no ideal hour for fallen love.*

*Indeed, how every moment seems so wrong.*

*Suppressed heart shadows milky moon above—*

*I watch the minutes flee; alone is near.*

*My hearts sings sad songs, too—but none to hear.*

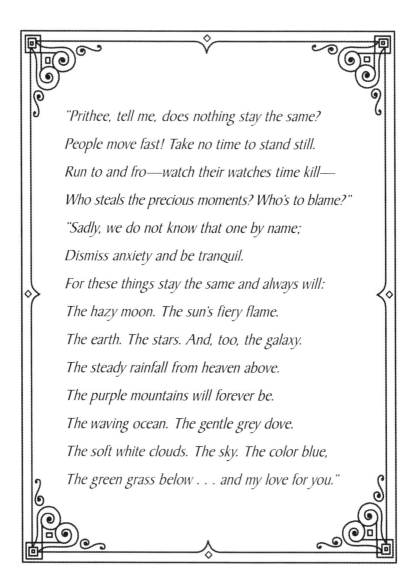

*"Prithee, tell me, does nothing stay the same?*
*People move fast! Take no time to stand still.*
*Run to and fro—watch their watches time kill—*
*Who steals the precious moments? Who's to blame?"*
*"Sadly, we do not know that one by name;*
*Dismiss anxiety and be tranquil.*
*For these things stay the same and always will:*
*The hazy moon. The sun's fiery flame.*
*The earth. The stars. And, too, the galaxy.*
*The steady rainfall from heaven above.*
*The purple mountains will forever be.*
*The waving ocean. The gentle grey dove.*
*The soft white clouds. The sky. The color blue,*
*The green grass below . . . and my love for you."*

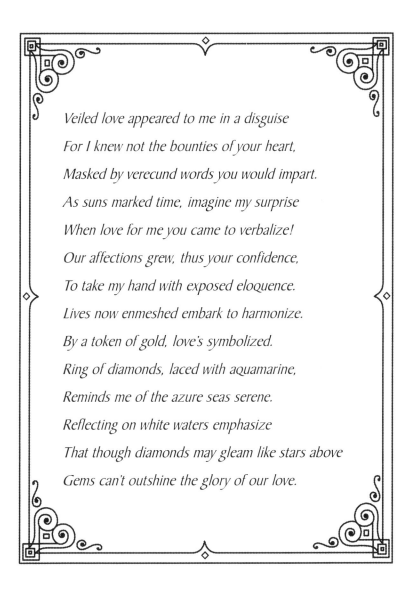

Veiled love appeared to me in a disguise

For I knew not the bounties of your heart,

Masked by verecund words you would impart.

As suns marked time, imagine my surprise

When love for me you came to verbalize!

Our affections grew, thus your confidence,

To take my hand with exposed eloquence.

Lives now enmeshed embark to harmonize.

By a token of gold, love's symbolized.

Ring of diamonds, laced with aquamarine,

Reminds me of the azure seas serene.

Reflecting on white waters emphasize

That though diamonds may gleam like stars above

Gems can't outshine the glory of our love.

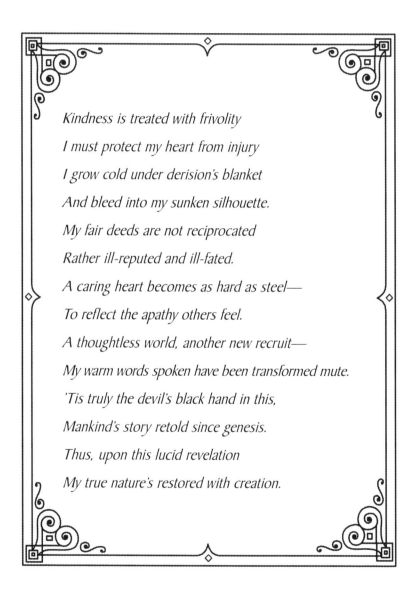

Kindness is treated with frivolity
I must protect my heart from injury
I grow cold under derision's blanket
And bleed into my sunken silhouette.
My fair deeds are not reciprocated
Rather ill-reputed and ill-fated.
A caring heart becomes as hard as steel—
To reflect the apathy others feel.
A thoughtless world, another new recruit—
My warm words spoken have been transformed mute.
'Tis truly the devil's black hand in this,
Mankind's story retold since genesis.
Thus, upon this lucid revelation
My true nature's restored with creation.

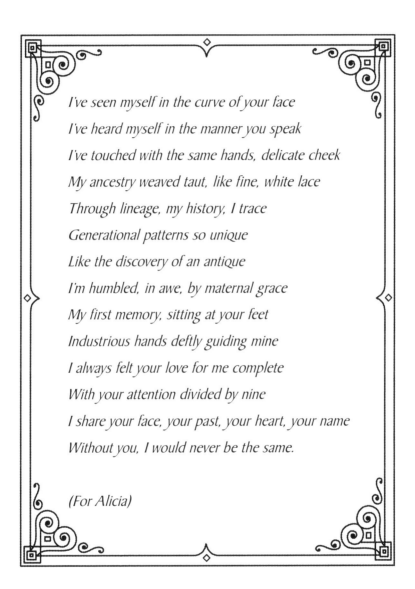

I've seen myself in the curve of your face
I've heard myself in the manner you speak
I've touched with the same hands, delicate cheek
My ancestry weaved taut, like fine, white lace
Through lineage, my history, I trace
Generational patterns so unique
Like the discovery of an antique
I'm humbled, in awe, by maternal grace
My first memory, sitting at your feet
Industrious hands deftly guiding mine
I always felt your love for me complete
With your attention divided by nine
I share your face, your past, your heart, your name
Without you, I would never be the same.

(For Alicia)

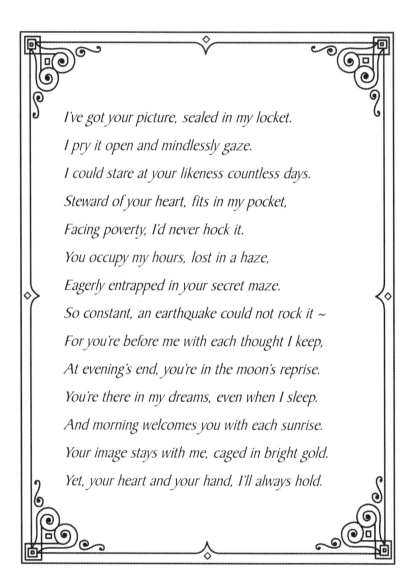

*I've got your picture, sealed in my locket.*

*I pry it open and mindlessly gaze.*

*I could stare at your likeness countless days.*

*Steward of your heart, fits in my pocket,*

*Facing poverty, I'd never hock it.*

*You occupy my hours, lost in a haze,*

*Eagerly entrapped in your secret maze.*

*So constant, an earthquake could not rock it ~*

*For you're before me with each thought I keep,*

*At evening's end, you're in the moon's reprise.*

*You're there in my dreams, even when I sleep.*

*And morning welcomes you with each sunrise.*

*Your image stays with me, caged in bright gold.*

*Yet, your heart and your hand, I'll always hold.*

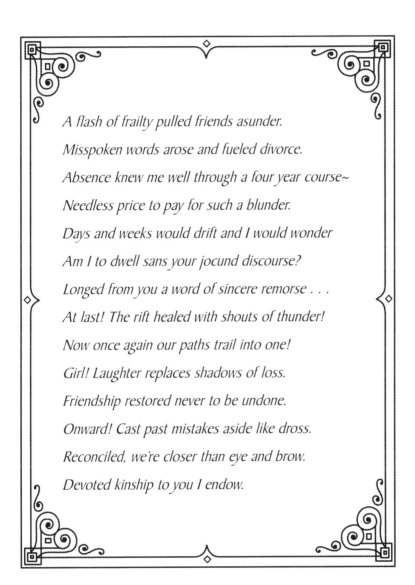

*A flash of frailty pulled friends asunder.*

*Misspoken words arose and fueled divorce.*

*Absence knew me well through a four year course~*

*Needless price to pay for such a blunder.*

*Days and weeks would drift and I would wonder*

*Am I to dwell sans your jocund discourse?*

*Longed from you a word of sincere remorse . . .*

*At last! The rift healed with shouts of thunder!*

*Now once again our paths trail into one!*

*Girl! Laughter replaces shadows of loss.*

*Friendship restored never to be undone.*

*Onward! Cast past mistakes aside like dross.*

*Reconciled, we're closer than eye and brow.*

*Devoted kinship to you I endow.*

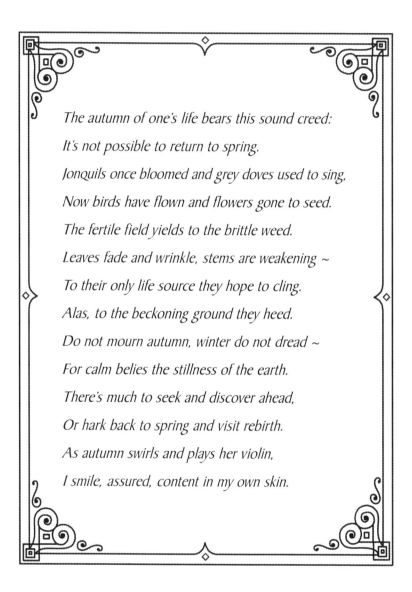

The autumn of one's life bears this sound creed:
It's not possible to return to spring.
Jonquils once bloomed and grey doves used to sing,
Now birds have flown and flowers gone to seed.
The fertile field yields to the brittle weed.
Leaves fade and wrinkle, stems are weakening ~
To their only life source they hope to cling.
Alas, to the beckoning ground they heed.
Do not mourn autumn, winter do not dread ~
For calm belies the stillness of the earth.
There's much to seek and discover ahead,
Or hark back to spring and visit rebirth.
As autumn swirls and plays her violin,
I smile, assured, content in my own skin.

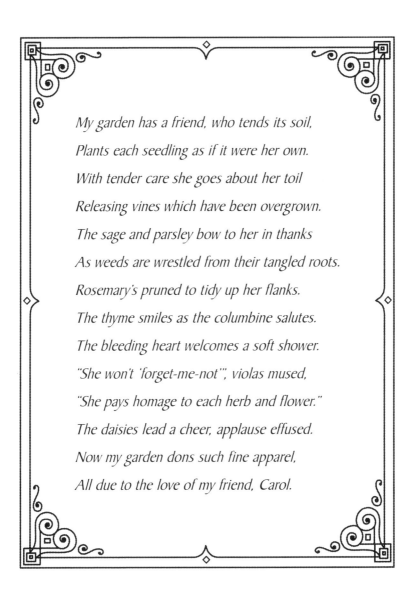

My garden has a friend, who tends its soil,

Plants each seedling as if it were her own.

With tender care she goes about her toil

Releasing vines which have been overgrown.

The sage and parsley bow to her in thanks

As weeds are wrestled from their tangled roots.

Rosemary's pruned to tidy up her flanks.

The thyme smiles as the columbine salutes.

The bleeding heart welcomes a soft shower.

"She won't 'forget-me-not'", violas mused,

"She pays homage to each herb and flower."

The daisies lead a cheer, applause effused.

Now my garden dons such fine apparel,

All due to the love of my friend, Carol.

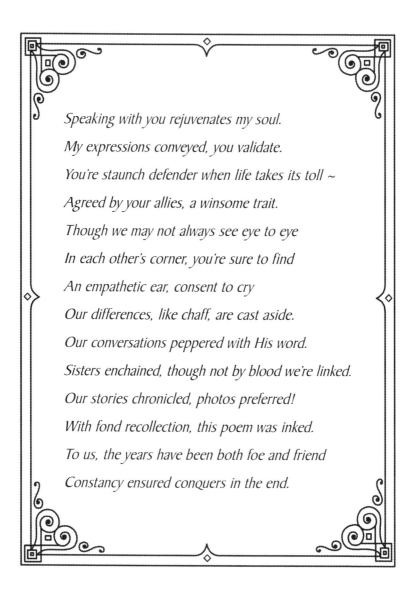

*Speaking with you rejuvenates my soul.*

*My expressions conveyed, you validate.*

*You're staunch defender when life takes its toll ~*

*Agreed by your allies, a winsome trait.*

*Though we may not always see eye to eye*

*In each other's corner, you're sure to find*

*An empathetic ear, consent to cry*

*Our differences, like chaff, are cast aside.*

*Our conversations peppered with His word.*

*Sisters enchained, though not by blood we're linked.*

*Our stories chronicled, photos preferred!*

*With fond recollection, this poem was inked.*

*To us, the years have been both foe and friend*

*Constancy ensured conquers in the end.*

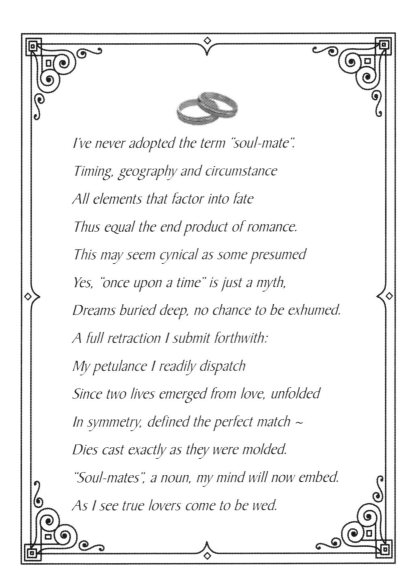

I've never adopted the term "soul-mate".

Timing, geography and circumstance

All elements that factor into fate

Thus equal the end product of romance.

This may seem cynical as some presumed

Yes, "once upon a time" is just a myth,

Dreams buried deep, no chance to be exhumed.

A full retraction I submit forthwith:

My petulance I readily dispatch

Since two lives emerged from love, unfolded

In symmetry, defined the perfect match ~

Dies cast exactly as they were molded.

"Soul-mates", a noun, my mind will now embed.

As I see true lovers come to be wed.

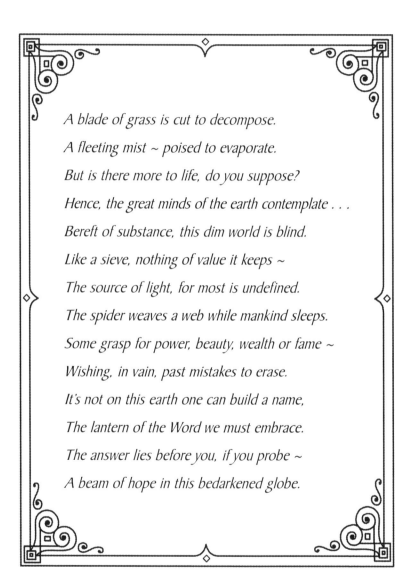

A blade of grass is cut to decompose.

A fleeting mist ~ poised to evaporate.

But is there more to life, do you suppose?

Hence, the great minds of the earth contemplate . . .

Bereft of substance, this dim world is blind.

Like a sieve, nothing of value it keeps ~

The source of light, for most is undefined.

The spider weaves a web while mankind sleeps.

Some grasp for power, beauty, wealth or fame ~

Wishing, in vain, past mistakes to erase.

It's not on this earth one can build a name,

The lantern of the Word we must embrace.

The answer lies before you, if you probe ~

A beam of hope in this bedarkened globe.

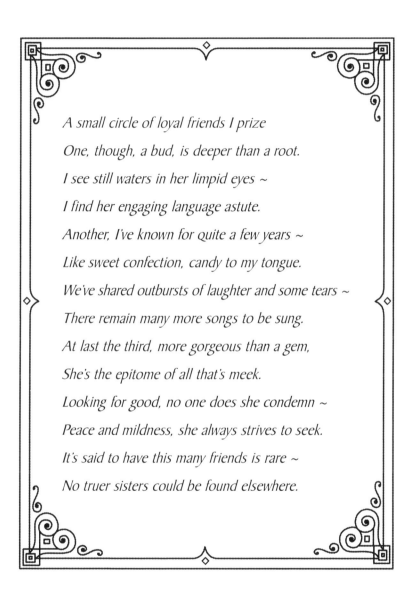

*A small circle of loyal friends I prize*

*One, though, a bud, is deeper than a root.*

*I see still waters in her limpid eyes ~*

*I find her engaging language astute.*

*Another, I've known for quite a few years ~*

*Like sweet confection, candy to my tongue.*

*We've shared outbursts of laughter and some tears ~*

*There remain many more songs to be sung.*

*At last the third, more gorgeous than a gem,*

*She's the epitome of all that's meek.*

*Looking for good, no one does she condemn ~*

*Peace and mildness, she always strives to seek.*

*It's said to have this many friends is rare ~*

*No truer sisters could be found elsewhere.*

*An unexpected concert met my ears ~*

*Never more upbeat lyrics had I heard.*

*Dancing melody with each song appears ~*

*Yarn entwines the chord with the written word.*

*Guitar strumming sounded just fine by me.*

*Rhythmically, the crowd was hypnotized*

*And ladies waved their hands in harmony.*

*"Miss me" kept the audience mesmerized.*

*Music composed while struggling showed us how*

*Easy it is to keep your head up high.*

*Recalling his roots keeps him grounded now ~*

*Resolved, his shield is raised to say good-bye.*

*Open-hearted, he gives his voice to throngs ~*

*X-rays exposed, he sees us through his songs.*

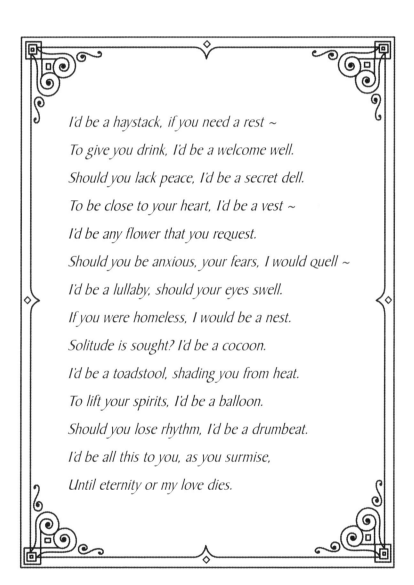

*I'd be a haystack, if you need a rest ~*

*To give you drink, I'd be a welcome well.*

*Should you lack peace, I'd be a secret dell.*

*To be close to your heart, I'd be a vest ~*

*I'd be any flower that you request.*

*Should you be anxious, your fears, I would quell ~*

*I'd be a lullaby, should your eyes swell.*

*If you were homeless, I would be a nest.*

*Solitude is sought? I'd be a cocoon.*

*I'd be a toadstool, shading you from heat.*

*To lift your spirits, I'd be a balloon.*

*Should you lose rhythm, I'd be a drumbeat.*

*I'd be all this to you, as you surmise,*

*Until eternity or my love dies.*

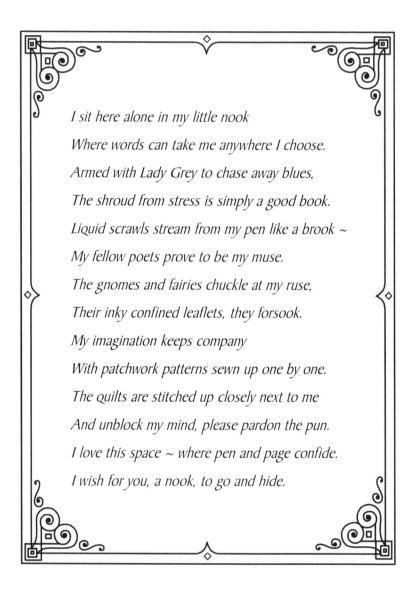

I sit here alone in my little nook

Where words can take me anywhere I choose.

Armed with Lady Grey to chase away blues,

The shroud from stress is simply a good book.

Liquid scrawls stream from my pen like a brook ~

My fellow poets prove to be my muse.

The gnomes and fairies chuckle at my ruse,

Their inky confined leaflets, they forsook.

My imagination keeps company

With patchwork patterns sewn up one by one.

The quilts are stitched up closely next to me

And unblock my mind, please pardon the pun.

I love this space ~ where pen and page confide.

I wish for you, a nook, to go and hide.

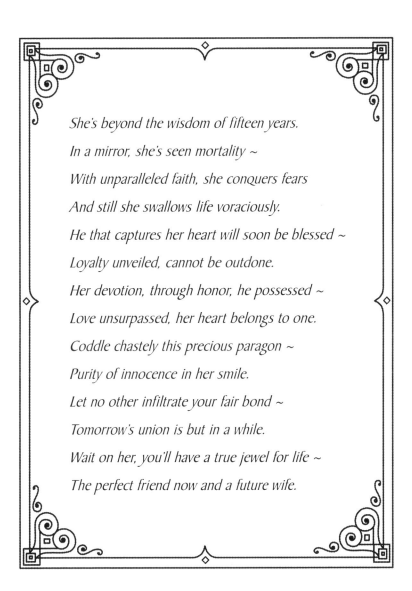

*She's beyond the wisdom of fifteen years.*

*In a mirror, she's seen mortality ~*

*With unparalleled faith, she conquers fears*

*And still she swallows life voraciously.*

*He that captures her heart will soon be blessed ~*

*Loyalty unveiled, cannot be outdone.*

*Her devotion, through honor, he possessed ~*

*Love unsurpassed, her heart belongs to one.*

*Coddle chastely this precious paragon ~*

*Purity of innocence in her smile.*

*Let no other infiltrate your fair bond ~*

*Tomorrow's union is but in a while.*

*Wait on her, you'll have a true jewel for life ~*

*The perfect friend now and a future wife.*

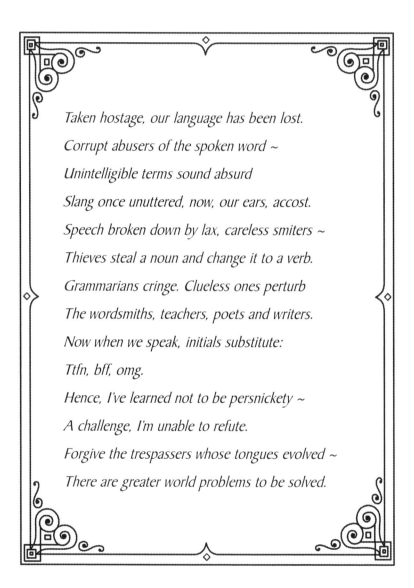

Taken hostage, our language has been lost.

Corrupt abusers of the spoken word ~

Unintelligible terms sound absurd

Slang once unuttered, now, our ears, accost.

Speech broken down by lax, careless smiters ~

Thieves steal a noun and change it to a verb.

Grammarians cringe. Clueless ones perturb

The wordsmiths, teachers, poets and writers.

Now when we speak, initials substitute:

Ttfn, bff, omg.

Hence, I've learned not to be persnickety ~

A challenge, I'm unable to refute.

Forgive the trespassers whose tongues evolved ~

There are greater world problems to be solved.

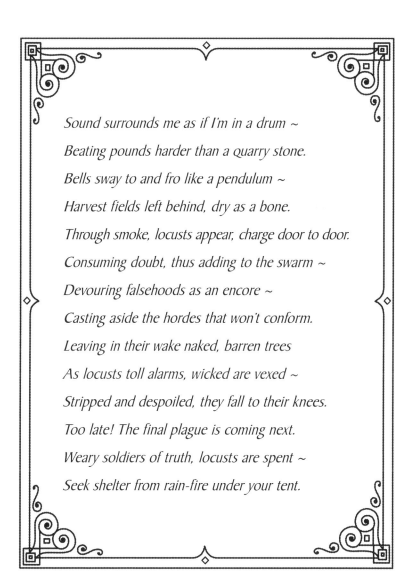

Sound surrounds me as if I'm in a drum ~

Beating pounds harder than a quarry stone.

Bells sway to and fro like a pendulum ~

Harvest fields left behind, dry as a bone.

Through smoke, locusts appear, charge door to door.

Consuming doubt, thus adding to the swarm ~

Devouring falsehoods as an encore ~

Casting aside the hordes that won't conform.

Leaving in their wake naked, barren trees

As locusts toll alarms, wicked are vexed ~

Stripped and despoiled, they fall to their knees.

Too late! The final plague is coming next.

Weary soldiers of truth, locusts are spent ~

Seek shelter from rain-fire under your tent.

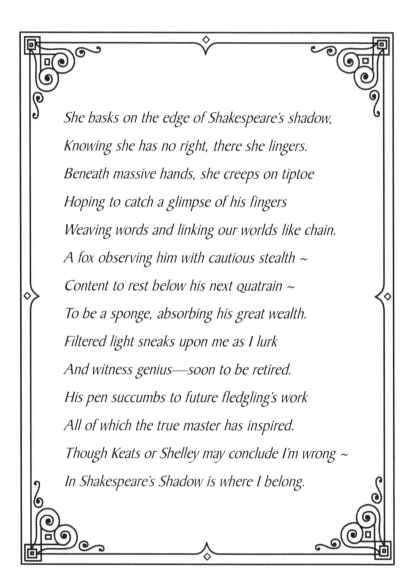

She basks on the edge of Shakespeare's shadow,
Knowing she has no right, there she lingers.
Beneath massive hands, she creeps on tiptoe
Hoping to catch a glimpse of his fingers
Weaving words and linking our worlds like chain.
A fox observing him with cautious stealth ~
Content to rest below his next quatrain ~
To be a sponge, absorbing his great wealth.
Filtered light sneaks upon me as I lurk
And witness genius—soon to be retired.
His pen succumbs to future fledgling's work
All of which the true master has inspired.
Though Keats or Shelley may conclude I'm wrong ~
In Shakespeare's Shadow is where I belong.

# About the Author

*Maria Tucciarone has a fervent admiration for the sonnet, her first love. She is a poet and a former English teacher. She was born in Willingboro, New Jersey and grew up in Richmond, Virginia. Later, she moved to Los Angeles, California where she met her husband, bass guitarist, Tom Tucciarone. After returning to her roots in Virginia, she left teaching to raise her two children. Currently, in the autumn of her life, she enjoys writing, gardening, antiquing and volunteering in Bible education work in her community. Her poetry has received Commendation in the 2009 Margaret Reid Poetry Prize for Traditional Verse.*

*The sonnet has been resuscitated in this illuminating treasure trove of poetry. In Shakespeare's Shadow is a rich collection of sonnets exploring a wide variety of topics such as love and romance, nature, family and friendship, faith, mortality, human struggle and more. The author captures her passion for iambic pentameter, acrostics, as well as, her mentor and inspiration, William Shakespeare. A perfect companion to a cup of tea and a moment of leisure, savor these sonnets and let your imagination drift into the shadows.*

# Author's Note

*To all those, too numerous to mention by name, who have inspired my sonnets, I thank you. I am indebted to my family for their constancy and support. Thanks to the publishers, coordinators and editors at Trafford for their time and assistance in getting this book in your hands. A nod of gratitude goes to Mark Davy, my fellow writer, for his critique and proofreading. And because I'm severely technologically challenged, profuse thanks goes to Brent Thayer, my computer tech guru, who through endless resources edited and basically handled the submission process for this book. I owe you!*